Texans Touched by World War II

Stephen Neal Manning

Republic of Texas Press
Plano, Texas

Library of Congress Cataloging-in-Publication Data

Texans touched by World War II / [interviewed by] Stephen Neal Manning.
   p. cm.
  ISBN 1-55622-942-9 (alk. paper)
  1. World War, 1939-1945--United States--Texas. 2. World War,
1939-1945--Personal narratives, American. 3. Texas--History,
Military. I. Manning, Stephen. II. Title: Texans touched by
World War 2. III. Title: Texans touched by World War Two.

D769.85.T4T48 2002
976.4'062--dc21   2002012827

Republic of Texas Press is an imprint of Wordware Publishing, Inc.
No part of this book may be reproduced in any form or by
any means without permission in writing from
Wordware Publishing, Inc.

Printed in the United States of America

ISBN 1-55622-942-9
10 9 8 7 6 5 4 3 2 1
0209

All inquiries for volume purchases of this book should be addressed to
Wordware Publishing, Inc., at 2320 Los Rios Boulevard, Plano, Texas 75074.
Telephone inquiries may be made by calling:

(972) 423-0090

Contents

Contents

Acknowledgments

Many thanks to the following individuals for their assistance in locating sources, arranging interviews, or collecting photographs: Toni Ewton, Charles Eck, Ava Moody, Jeannie Surber, Chris Manning, Neil Gibson, Debbie Juern, Dennis Brand of the American Legion, and my wife, Maria.

Introduction

I sit here in 91 degrees struggling to finish this book. My forehead, the back of my neck, and the sides of my stomach distract me with a disagreeable wetness. I try to concentrate on words and ignore the warmth pressing in on me. Whenever I shift in the chair I feel my damp clothes and for that matter, my skin, sticking to vinyl. I'm sure I stink.

My air conditioning has broken down in the last week of July. Any sane person would leave the house and go to a movie or a swimming pool. But I am not a sane person. I am a writer who has a deadline to meet. So I stick it out at my computer, gulping down cold water and deriving what little cool air I can from three valiant but outmatched fans. As if that weren't bad enough, my computer refuses to cooperate. It keeps crashing at apparently random times—sometimes when I push a button on the keyboard, and sometimes when I'm not even touching the keyboard. I restart the computer, over and over.

The lack of air conditioning is an anomaly in my life, one that is hard to wrap my mind around. I keep thinking about one of the veterans in this book, Buddy Lewis, who told me what it was like living in Washington, D.C., where he worked during the summer of 1941 before the U.S. entered World War II. "I lived in a little room on the third floor of a rooming house, and when I woke up in the morning I would be lying in a small lake of sweat. The entire bed would be soaked. Man, this was back when. And you don't want to think about when."

Such was life before air conditioning became common. I've had to live without it three days now and have one more to go before it will be fixed. But at least I have an air conditioning unit to fix; I can't imagine having to live without it because it doesn't exist. And I curse this uncooperative computer, but where would I be without it? A book like this, which involves finding and contacting people over great distances, would be much harder to accomplish without my connection to the Internet.

Then I realize I am experiencing a small slice (a tiny little sliver, a microscopic particle, really) of life during the 1940s. I have been given a small window into another era. I can just begin to imagine myself wearing a wool Army uniform all day in this heat. I can just begin to imagine what it felt like below decks aboard a Liberty ship filled to the brim with men emitting body heat and odors. For them, there was no relief on the way from such discomforts. That was just the way it was.

One thing's for sure, I wouldn't want to live back then. I prefer looking at worldwide conflict from a safe distance, and I'm too dependent on the everyday luxuries we enjoy today. Especially air conditioning. Disposable diapers are nice, too. If I could travel back in time, it would be a short visit with a return ticket. But even so, isn't it interesting to know what people lived through back then?

History is a fascinating subject if taught in a way that makes it relevant. Unfortunately that's often not the way it's taught. My memory of history classes in high school and college is of bleary-eyed students struggling to maintain consciousness in the face of an unrelenting barrage of dates and statistics. Sound familiar? We could hardly do more to make history dull if we tried. No one ever asks or answers the question of why memorizing dates is so important.

When we make history uninviting, we steer people's minds away from its lessons. History is more than a series of dates to be memorized. History is the story of people doing the best they can with the circumstances in which they live. And the way to benefit from it is to understand what it was like for the people who lived through it.

It may be difficult to imagine yourself in the shoes of a primitive man in the Ice Age or a citizen of the Roman Empire, but in the case of World War II we've got a golden opportunity—for the time being. Between four and five million World War II veterans still live in the United States today, along with millions more of their family members old enough to remember that era. Each one of these people is a walking, talking search engine, the next best thing to a time machine, because they can sit down with us and bring a different era to life for us if we are willing to listen.

Their knowledge is especially relevant now, as our nation wakes up from a long, sweet dream to the reality that the far corners of the world harbor fanatics who fantasize of killing Americans and are capable of doing it. We all lived through September 11, 2001, but for the World War II generation, it wasn't a new experience. They had already seen Pearl Harbor. Asked to compare the two, the people featured in this book saw many parallels: the sudden realization that there are people out there in the world who hate us; the puzzlement over why anybody would want to harm us; and the quick bonding together as Americans in the wake of a national tragedy.

But, for all the similarities, there were some major differences. As Neil and Toni Gibson of Arlington told me, the change in people's lives after Pearl Harbor was a thousand times greater than the effects of September 11 on people's day-to-day routine. And the surge in patriotism after Pearl Harbor didn't fade in a few months as it did in 2001; it lasted for years.

This book portrays something most living Americans have never seen, even in the wake of September 11: total war, a conflict that touches every one of us. After Pearl Harbor the country found itself immersed in a war in which every civilian, even the children, played a supporting role. In the midst of our shadowy war on terrorism, most of us go about our daily lives as if nothing ever happened. Even now, after the darkest day most of us can remember, we do not have to live with rationing of food, clothing, and gasoline, and the overwhelming majority of us don't have to live with the worry that a son, father, or husband in the military won't come home alive.

The lesson of history is that as bad as September 11, 2001 was, our nation has been through dark times before and ended up stronger than ever before. The heroism we witnessed in New York City and at the Pentagon, and the liberation of a hostage population in Afghanistan, provided glimpses of what Americans have always done in difficult times. We *rebound*.

The Texans featured in this book tell stories that illustrate how different life was sixty years ago, when luxuries were scarce but families were strong, when making a living was hard work but neighbors helped each other, when life moved at a slower pace but people had time for each other. Sit back and let yourself be transported through time. Ask yourself: How would you handle the challenges they faced in everyday life?

Hatred will never go away, and the strong possibility remains that we may suffer more days like September 11, 2001. But we have a blueprint for how to cope. In difficult times, we should follow the example of the World War II generation, our experts on adjusting to hardship and facing down evil. We should live up to our responsibilities, even when they (gasp!) inconvenience us. We should get to know our neighbors and help them when they are in need. We should be willing to do without the luxuries to which we're accustomed. We should think of the greater good, rather than our own self-interest. We should remember: Our finest hour always follows our darkest. And we are at our best when things are at their worst.

They shoved me aside to wash
the blood off their bayonets

Louis Read
Dallas

I opened my front door, wondering what to expect. I looked my visitor over and searched his face for souvenirs from a return trip to hell. An eighty-one-year-old man stood before me with a half-smile and a hardened gaze from eyes that had seen things beyond my imagination.

His name was Louis Read. He had come to talk about Bataan.

Bataan.

In the realm of emotionally loaded words, this one is heavy artillery. According to cartographers it's a peninsula in the Philippines. But for the haunted fraternity of men who defended it fiercely until their capture, the word has other meanings: Horror. Desperation. Cruelty.

I had asked Reed to relive his days as a prisoner of the Japanese during World War II. It's hard to imagine an existence more remote from the comfortable lives we lead today. Each time I enter this world of memories, I must steel myself.

1

Louis Read as a young man.

Read and I shook hands and I offered him something to drink; he politely declined. We did not spend much time on small talk. He wanted to dive into the story.

We sat at the kitchen table and I listened intently, ignoring the high-pitched barking of my Dalmatian, Cookie, who was indignant at being left in the backyard rather than allowed inside to jump all over my guest and carpet his slacks with white hairs.

"I served in a rifle company in the National Guard while I attended Pleasant Grove High School, a little rural school outside Dallas," Read began. His voice was low and gruff. "I had to go to downtown Dallas to drill every Wednesday night, so I'd wear my uniform to school that day and then I'd walk six miles to the National Guard unit. That was my only source of income. I got paid one dollar every time I drilled, and every three months I got a check for $12. That was big money then." He grinned, but I noticed, as I would notice many times during the interview, that the grin did not reach his eyes.

"I joined the Army in June 1939. An uncle and a cousin of mine both graduated from West Point in the thirties, and they wanted me to go there too. I passed the physical and academic requirements, but I couldn't get an appointment. I didn't have the political connections. So I enlisted in the Army and went to West Point Preparatory School to try to get in that way. That school had 250 enlisted men vying for four slots at West Point. Most of the people I competed against were sons of generals. I lasted until they had cut us down to 75 men and then I got washed out.

"I ended up in the 9th Infantry Regiment of the 2nd Division and became a rifle squad leader. We went on maneuvers in January 1941, 60 miles south of San Antonio. Believe it or not, a blizzard blew up and lasted a week."

"In south Texas?" I asked.

"That's right. Bitter cold, heavy snow. My buddy Marion Terrell from Deputy, Indiana, sat with me in the middle of a plowed field where they had set up a movie screen. We watched a GI movie about the Philippine Islands. We saw palm trees and people walking around in white linen suits. Then we looked at the snow around us, and we said, 'To hell with this, let's go to the tropics.' We immediately decided to apply for foreign service." He chuckled.

"When you went on foreign service you had to stay two years minimum. Our enlistments would have been up before then, so they said we had to take a discharge and re-enlist as buck privates in order to go. So that's what we did. We arrived in Manila on April 22, 1941."

"What did you think of the Philippines?" I asked.

"I loved it. That was the best duty I ever saw in the Army before the war. The weather was good, and every-thing was cheap. Right after I arrived, I got a chance to take a job as a company clerk for an anti-tank company in the 31st Infantry Regiment. I jumped at it. I didn't like paper-work, but it doubled my pay just like that, from twenty-one to forty-two dollars a month. We worked in the morning, took siesta in the afternoon, and went out on the town at night. We had lots of bars to go to. We could also go watch jai alai.

"The tiny little taxicabs cost seven centavos to ride. They burned alcohol instead of gasoline. Sugar's a big crop there, and the Filipinos made alcohol out of it, and it pro-vided them with an abundant fuel. We had Chinese tailors

4

make us white Irish linen suits to wear off duty. Cost six bucks to get one made. We had our fatigues and even our shoes tailor-made, for crying out loud! A Filipino would come around and measure our feet and make shoes for us. Didn't cost much at all.

"We didn't have to do any KP or make up our own bunks. We hired Filipinos to do it all and took up a collection to pay them. Each of us put in three pesos a month."

He shook his head in chagrin. "Funny thing happened: I belonged to an NCO club that was in an old Victorian-style mansion, and we could go out there and get our meals and run up a tab. One thing that still gripes me is I went there the night before Pearl Harbor and paid my 150-peso bill. The next day that place got blown off the map!"

"Should have waited," I observed.

"Yeah, I still think about that!" he said with a quick, truncated laugh.

"Tell me about some of your buddies," I suggested.

"Two men from the 2nd Division went over there with me: Marion Terrell and Leon Beck. Terrell died in 1949, Beck died in 2000. But all three of us made it back from the prison camps, and that's a rare thing. They say the death rate among American prisoners in German camps was around 1 percent, and among prisoners in Japanese camps, nearly 40 percent. My regiment lost 70 percent total, including those killed in combat, but most of them died as a result of being prisoners of war. It's a miracle that both my friends and I made it back. Out of 150 in my company, three of us are alive today."

"What do you remember about the beginning of the war?"

"The Japanese attacked Pearl Harbor on December 7, but because of the time zone difference it was December 8 in the Philippines. We got word about Pearl Harbor on the radio early that morning. Nobody knew what to think or what to do. That whole day we stood still and waited for orders, and none came. The next day our commanders ordered us out of our barracks at Fort McKinley. We were right behind Nichols Field, a fighter base, and they ordered us to dig foxholes around the perimeter to protect the runway. We sat out there, waiting, but all was quiet.

"Late that night I decided I'd had enough of my foxhole and returned to the barracks and climbed into my bunk. Around midnight a large explosion blew me out of the bed. I thought, 'Earthquake!'

"But it wasn't an earthquake. Japanese high-level bombers flew overhead and bombed the Pan American Airways radio station, right next to our barracks.

"Our regiment moved out to Lingayen Gulf where we expected the Japanese to land. They left me behind in charge of guarding and maintaining the barracks. On December 10 I heard the air raid siren, grabbed my M-1 rifle and a full belt of ammunition, and ran out behind the barracks. I lay on my back in a ditch, looking up at the sky. Above me I saw more bombers and Zero fighters than I could count.

"Soon every building at Nichols Field was in flames. I watched our airplanes sitting on the tarmac explode one by one. The Zeroes circled repeatedly, flying low and fast and strafing everything in sight. I fired five or six clips at them with the M-1 but I doubt I hit anything. Those things moved too fast to get a good lead on them.

"With Nichols Field destroyed I had no reason to remain there. I made my way to the main line of resistance the American and Filipino armies had hastily set up on the Bataan Peninsula, arriving on Christmas Eve. Our Christmas dinner consisted of two slices of cold potato and a cup of cold coffee. Food was scarce because the Army was so disorganized. In fact, we were in a state of chaos. It seemed like everybody in the Philippines was converging on us, trying to get into Bataan behind our line.

"My company had obsolete 37mm guns and one platoon of one-pound howitzers with wooden wheels from World War I. I was the only man in the company who had ever seen a live round for the 37mm guns. By the way, the Japanese tanks had 47mm guns.

"In late January the Japanese made their big push to wipe us out. They attacked us at Abucay Hacienda, crossing rice paddies and getting mowed down by our machine guns and artillery, which held the high ground. Then they tried to get around by landing troops on the west side of the peninsula behind our line, but our units in the rear repelled them each time. We held out much longer than anyone, certainly the Japanese, expected. But our food supplies were critically low; we were hungry all the time. We searched the jungles and banana plantations for anything to eat. More and more men fell ill with malaria or dysentery. We could pick up radio stations from San Francisco, and we listened to them praising us for holding out so long and promising us that troops, tanks, and planes were on the way to relieve us. They weren't.

"When the main battle came, the Japs got artillery observation on us from a high vantage point by running up a barrage balloon from a truck. A man sat in a basket hanging underneath and watched us with a telescope. We could all see it behind their lines, too far for us to shoot it down. They'd reel it in every night and put it back up the next day.

"Once they started doing that, the frequency, intensity, and accuracy of their artillery barrages increased. They had complete air superiority and bombed and strafed us from the air. The Filipino divisions disintegrated in the bombardment, and our units became disorganized soon after."

Read slowed down and began to speak with quiet intensity.

"When things fell apart for us during the battle that followed," he said, looking down at the table, "I got separated from my outfit. I didn't know where I was. Everybody just disappeared in the dark, and I found myself all alone. I was in a tiny clearing in the jungle, late in the evening. I heard Japs all around me, jabbering. I sat quietly on the ground hoping they'd all pass by. I held my rifle with its butt against the ground, with a fixed bayonet pointing upward at a 45-degree angle.

"All of a sudden a Jap jumped out of the bushes at me, screaming his lungs out. Scared the hell out of me. He landed right on my bayonet and fell dead. I pulled the dang thing out. Of course the noise alerted the other Japs, and they swarmed around me. One got in behind me and bayoneted me right here." He touched his left side, towards the back.

"I fell to the ground and didn't move. Evidently they were in a hurry, because they just assumed I was dead and went on. But the bayonet didn't hit anything vital. I had a bleeding hole in my side, so I tore a piece of cloth off my shirt and stuffed the cloth in the hole to stop the flow. I decided I'd better try to get back to the field hospital. I walked a long way through jungle, heading back in the general direction of the field hospital. The next day a sniper shot me through the helmet and grazed my scalp. I ducked down out of sight behind a tree and then went on my way, bleeding like a stuck pig.

"Eventually I reached a mango grove and went in there and sat down to rest. Those huge trees are excellent hiding places for tanks and trucks, so whenever the Japanese pilots saw a mango grove they'd automatically bomb it. I was the only living thing in the mango grove except for the mango ants, and sure enough a Jap dive bomber passed over and dropped a bomb. Several pieces of shrapnel hit me. One hit me on the bridge of the nose and broke it; my nose is still broken to this day. I've got some scars, like this one right here on my nose.

"I still have a piece of scrap iron come out of me now and then, believe it or not. A couple of years ago I looked at the mirror one morning, getting ready to shave, and I had a big black bump right here." He pointed to a spot just in front of his right ear. "I thought, my God, I've got a melanoma. I started picking at it with a sterilized needle and out came a piece of black metal!

"I was now bleeding from my side, my scalp, and all the shrapnel wounds and was beginning to worry about loss of blood. Fortunately, I found my way back to the field hospital at a place called Little Baguio. The Japs hadn't bothered it yet. I lined up with a lot of other people there for about an hour and finally got to a medic. By then many of my wounds had stopped bleeding. He sprinkled sulfa powder everywhere and dressed the obvious wounds and sent me on my way."

"Where did you go?"

"I just kept walking, hoping to escape to Corregidor and get the hell out of there. I headed for the beach, thinking I might be able to swim across to the island, but I discovered the Japs were already on the beach. A number of people from my regiment did make it to Corregidor, and several men I knew personally got killed over there when the Japs landed on the island.

"I retreated into the jungle and wandered past a town called Mariveles on the tip of Bataan then continued around to the mountains on the west side of the peninsula. I saw a lot of stragglers I didn't know. I worked my way up a dirt road onto Signal Hill and ran into a bunch of people, officers mostly, hiding out. We'd been ordered to surrender on the 9th of April, and these people were waiting around to be taken prisoner. But I met up with a friend from a different company in my regiment, a guy named James Dunn from McKinney, Texas, and we decided we were gonna head for the hills. To hell with surrendering!

"We gathered rifles, a pistol, ammunition, and a couple cans of salmon we found. We set out for the hills. Those jungle mountains were almost impassable, so we figured they'd be a good place to hide. But a lieutenant stopped us and asked where we were going, and we told him.

"He said, 'You're crazy. The Japanese have agreed to abide by the Geneva Convention on the treatment of prisoners, and everyone thinks the war will be over in three or four weeks anyway. You'll probably get malaria out there if you don't have it already.'

"I was one of the few who didn't already have malaria at that time. That's one thing that saved my life. I don't think I could have survived what was to come if I'd had malaria.

"Dunn and I talked it over and said, 'Well, if it's only going to last three or four more weeks, we can stand that, I guess,' so we decided to go with the rest of them. An American major arrived in a bus, loaded us up, and took us down to the Japs in Mariveles.

"Thousands of American soldiers milled around there, along with thousands of Filipino soldiers and civilians. The Japs segregated the Americans from the Filipinos, and they made us strip and they searched us. We had to stand around two or three days for repeated strip-searches. The Japs took everything except a mess kit and a canteen.

"I'd had some souvenirs I'd taken off dead Japs, like a Jap field manual, but I'd had enough sense to throw those away. I tossed them out into the jungle on the way down there. But lots of people still had their souvenirs, Japanese mess kits and occupation money, and when the Japanese found them, they turned the offenders over to a soldier with a rifle and a bayonet, sent them off, and we never saw them again. Nobody got away with that.

"Finally the Japs lined us up and started to march us. We'd had nothing to eat for several days. They lined us up in a column four across, about 2,000 men in our column, and told us we would march up to Balanga, the provincial capital, farther up the Bataan Peninsula. They told us, 'March to Balanga and you will be fed.'

"We stopped to rest only when the Jap guards wanted to rest. We'd just sit down in the middle of the road for a short time. We followed a narrow asphalt road that goes up the length of Bataan from Mariveles. As we marched toward Balanga, a constant flow of Jap soldiers streamed down the road in the other direction. Cavalry, tanks, you name it. Artillery—man, they had a lot of artillery. I soon found out the thing to do when they put us in a column of four was to get on the inside lane, because the Japs passing by in the other direction would whack people on the out-side lane over the head with their rifle butts. The ones on horseback were the worst about it.

"We made it to Balanga. They didn't feed us. But getting water was our most immediate problem. It was the hot and dry season; dust was everywhere. We passed bluffs on the side of the road and saw water coming out of cracks in the rock, and we tried to dart over there and fill our canteens. The Jap guards knelt down and shot at us whenever we did that, but they were pretty poor shots and I never did get hit. I'm sure some others did.

"Soon carabao wallows became our only source of water. A carabao is a water buffalo, a beast of burden that wallows in muddy water holes. We had to resort to drinking from those. Fortunately I had found a bottle of iodine lying on the ground, and I knew from my high school biology teacher you can sterilize water with iodine. So every time I got some water in my canteen from a spring or a buffalo wallow, I'd pour a little iodine in it and shake it up. I'm sure it helped. There's no tellin' what was in that water.

"We marched from town to town, and they never fed us. I understand some groups got some rice on the way but we didn't. We passed banana groves, but prisoners passing by ahead of us had completely eaten the trees. There were no trees left. I found a wild turnip or two that I dug up and ate. That's about all I had to eat the whole trip."

"You got bayoneted," I said, "and then had to walk 70 miles. How did you manage to do it?"

He shrugged. "The bayonet didn't hit anything of importance. I had bigger problems. The problem, even more than the distance, was the lack of food and water. We also had no shelter at night, and we couldn't break ranks for any reason, not even to pee or crap. The men with dysentery just crapped all over themselves as they walked. I didn't have that problem because I never had anything to eat in the first place."

"Could you tell me more about the condition of the men around you?" I asked.

"Well, some had malaria and a lot had dysentery. I didn't have either at that time, luckily. When a man has tertian malaria, he runs chills and fever every third day. Falciparum malaria is a lot worse; the fever is constant. These guys who had malaria or dysentery, they just couldn't keep going. We tried to keep them up on their feet, or a couple of us got together and tried to carry them. But eventually we just couldn't do it anymore and had to let them go. They'd fall back in the column, and as soon as they did, the Jap guards executed them on the spot, usually by bayoneting them. Occasionally an officer would chop their heads off with a sword."

I was struck by the contrast between his matter-of-fact tone and the brutal memory he was resurrecting with his words.

"How did the guards behave as they did this?" I asked. "Were they revolted by the orders they had been given?

Was it just a routine matter of following orders? Or did they actually enjoy it?"

Louis Read fixed me with a piercing stare. "I wouldn't be here today," he said harshly, "if it weren't for this fact: the Japanese soldiers would pass up a chance to shoot you any day if they thought they had a chance to stick a bayonet in you. Most of them were poor shots, but they loved knives, bayonets, and swords. I remember a couple of occasions during the fighting where they could have shot me, but they preferred to try to get closer and bayonet me.

"I heard of one instance at Ft. Santiago in September 1943 in which nineteen American officers and enlisted men got their heads chopped off simultaneously by Japanese officers with swords. One American witnessed it, and they let him go to tell the tale."

"Why did they kill them?" I asked.

Whenever I talk to men who were prisoners of the Japanese, I have a tendency to ask why their captors did the things they did. Call me naïve, but I can't help wanting a reason. Perhaps I'm trying to make sense out of senseless actions. But the answer I get is invariably the same.

"I *don't know*," Read said, shaking his head slowly, almost glaring at me. "Who knows what their reasons were? That was one of the biggest problems of being a prisoner of the Japanese. You lived with the awareness, every moment of every day, that you might be subject to summary execution for no reason at all, no matter where you were or what you were doing. It was an incredibly stressful existence. The Japs required us, even our officers, to bow and scrape to the lowliest Japanese buck private. They degraded us at every opportunity.

"Eventually we marched to a place called Lubao. A big corrugated steel warehouse stood there, filled with and surrounded by American prisoners. Must have been 5,000 of us in the compound. The Japs were cutting the columns down in size here to make them more controllable. I stayed there several days. We had one water hydrant for all the men, and I spent all my time lined up trying to get my canteen filled with water. We'd wait in line all day.

"One day I had almost made it up to the hydrant, maybe ten or twelve people ahead of me in line. Here came an old Jap officer, a stereotypical college prep-looking Jap with glasses so thick they looked like the bottoms of soda bottles. He strode right up and plucked the guy just in front of me out of line, a tall, handsome man with a mustache and a khaki overseas cap with Signal Corps piping on it. A real good-looking guy. He didn't do anything to cause trouble, but the Jap officer yanked him out of the line and turned him over to several soldiers, and I watched them take him across the road, tie him to a tree, and bayonet him."

The announcement was so sudden, the word spoken so darkly, I believe I may have visibly flinched.

"They threw his body into a bamboo clump. Then they came back just as I got up to the hydrant, and they shoved me aside to wash the blood off their bayonets."

What do you ask a man telling a story like this? I floundered, searching for something appropriate, but all I could come up with was the crutch of the run-of-the-mill TV reporter:

"How did you feel about it?" I asked.

"I was pretty scared. But I hadn't eaten in so long, hunger was the main thing on my mind, and everyone else's."

"Was this execution done simply for entertainment?" I pressed, still feeling a need for a reason.

"I have a theory about it," Read said thoughtfully. "This was the ugliest Jap you ever saw, short and real squirrelly looking, and the American was tall and handsome. I think that's why the Jap did it. Pure meanness because the American was everything the Jap wasn't."

I chewed on that for a moment. Louis Read collected his thoughts and continued.

"At this same camp at Lubao, I looked around one day and saw fifteen or twenty dead men laid out in a row. The Japs had put a bunch of Filipinos to work digging a hole and shoving the bodies in several at a time. Among the bodies, I recognized one of those good friends I'd come over with, Leon Beck. I said, 'My God, Beck's had it.'

"But after the war he showed up on my front porch one day!

"Turned out he had malaria and slipped into a coma, and later he woke up and found himself in the hole. He got up and out of there fast! He joined the march leaving the camp, watched for an opportunity, and escaped. When he saw no Japanese guards looking, he crawled into a culvert under the road and waited two or three days until everyone had passed by. Later he met up with Filipino guerrillas and spent the rest of the war with them. By the time he got back after the war, he had married a Filipino girl and had two kids.

"Finally my group reached Camp O'Donnell. People started dying like flies. We had plenty of American doctors, but they had no medical supplies to work with. Practically everybody I knew died there. James Dunn, the man I had planned to hide in the hills with, died the week after we got there. In the first two months at O'Donnell, 1,600 American prisoners died. Thousands and thousands of Filipinos died in a nearby camp."

"What was your condition like by now? Did you get malaria then?"

"Not yet. I was lucky. But something was going around called Japanese B encephalitis, and it killed a lot of men. Sometimes people I knew would get a headache at 3 o'clock in the afternoon, which was the first sign, and by 10 o'clock at night they were dead.

"I decided if I didn't get the hell out of there I was gonna die too. So I volunteered for a work detail. The Japs took us to the docks in Manila, and we unloaded rice from the hold of a ship, carrying 100-kilogram bags on our backs."

"How much is that in pounds?" I asked.

"That's 220 pounds."

"How did you manage to carry that, in your condition?" I asked skeptically.

"The bags were square in shape," he explained. "I bent over with my back parallel to the floor, and two people placed the bag on my back. Then I walked in that position until I unloaded the bag. I always had and still have very powerful legs. I guess they come from a lifetime of walking and running a lot. Remember I told you I walked six miles to get to drill practice back in high school. I also ran the mile in high school track, and in the infantry I went on a lot of hikes, carrying a full pack and rifle. Every day I give thanks for the good physical condition I was in before I went overseas.

"The next work detail I joined, we got on trucks without knowing where we were going. To my absolute horror, we went back down to Bataan, the last place I wanted to go. For a couple months we salvaged ammunition dumps that had been blown up. The rainy season had begun, and we had to sleep in pouring rain, lying on the ground. We had no tents. But we got fed every day. They fed us a dried, salted fish that had been split open, and some rice.

"At one point I realized we were no more than a kilometer from where I'd ended up on Signal Hill. I thought, 'By God I'm gonna sneak away from here if I get half a chance,' because I'd buried 1,600 pesos up there that I'd won playing blackjack. I wanted to get my hands on that because if I got back into prison camp with money, I could buy stuff with it. I was getting ready to go and try to retrieve the money and I got sick. I was lying down and suddenly found I couldn't get up.

"They had a tent for sick people to lie in, and I lay in there I don't know how long. I was out of my head, just vaguely aware of things going on around me. It turned out I had two kinds of malaria at the same time, and in addition to that I got infectious hepatitis. At that time they didn't know what that was, they just called it jaundice. An epidemic of it was going around, turning everybody canary yellow. After the war I was trained as a microbiologist, and that's how I know what it was. Now they call it hepatitis A. I was extremely weak and had to be lifted up onto the truck. Couldn't do anything. And I had been a pretty strong, healthy guy.

"We went back to Cabanatuan, their main prison camp in the Philippines. I stayed there almost a year and a half. I ran into Corregidor people there. They'd been trucked up from Bilibid Prison after being marched through the streets of Manila. Some of those Corregidor guys still had their footlockers with them, for crying out loud! Their officers still had their West Point rings, fountain pens, wrist watches. The Japs hadn't taken them. So the officers could sell that stuff in the camp. The Japs would pay pretty good money for them, and the prisoners could buy food with the money they made. Well, I didn't have anything to sell. I damn near died in there.

"A guy in my camp told me, 'We should sneak out through the barbed wire at night and go down to the barrio there and we can get all the cigarettes and stuff we want.' He wanted me to go with him. I would have, but I was just too damn sick; I couldn't go. That night the men who went got caught by the Japs and were executed. I narrowly escaped that. If I'd been in slightly better health, I'd have gone with them.

"My old first sergeant was a prisoner there, and he came around to see me. His name was Emanuel Hamburger. He'd been in the Army a long time. He'd been in China, the Mexican border campaign. All the officers regarded him with awe. The camp had a hospital across the road, and if you felt ready to die, you were supposed to go turn yourself in there. I was just about ready to turn myself in. Then I ran into Hamburger.

"I had been forced to carry bodies for burial details, a job I was not up to in my condition. Hamburger had a job inside the camp as a runner for a major in the camp administration. The Japs let our own officers run things inside the camp, subject to certain rules.

"Hamburger told me, 'I'll take you over to see my boss and see if we can get you a job inside the camp so you don't have to go out on burial detail.' I saw the major—talk about coincidences. It was Maj. John Neiger, a man I had known when he was a second lieutenant right out of West Point. Back then he was green as a gourd and I had helped him out some, so he owed me a favor. He gave me a job inside the camp, working for the supply department. My job, which I was barely able to handle, was to sit on the ground outside the window of an officers' building with a five-gallon lard bucket with a wooden handle. Once a day I took that bucket up a little hill to a hydrant and filled it with water and brought it back down for the officers. This took me all day, because I had to sit down and rest every few feet. The officers had ways of getting a little extra food, and they'd give me some scraps, so I ate a little better than I would have otherwise, and I gradually got better. Eventually I got healthy enough to carry rice sacks on my back again.

"In September of 1943 I went down to Manila Bay with a work detail of 800 prisoners to build an airfield for the Japanese. It's where Manila International Airport is now. We built one big, long runway over the course of a year. The Japanese used Filipinos to do the surveying, and we Americans would move the rock over from the high areas to the low areas to level the ground where the runway would go. When the Jap guards weren't nearby, the Filipinos would ask us Americans, 'How deep do you want to dig here, Joe?' They called everybody Joe, see. And we would show them with our hands, 'Oh, about this far,' and they would drive stakes into the ground to whatever level we told them! The Japanese had no idea what was going on. The result was, after the Japs concreted the runway, it looked something like this!" He swept his hand in front of him, rolling it up and down to indicate troughs and ridges. "The first plane that landed on that runway broke the concrete!"

We laughed. I was impressed. After all the Japanese had done to break the spirits of Read and the other prisoners, they still managed to sabotage something as significant as an airfield.

"A year later they moved us to Japan because the Americans were moving closer. We'd had an American air strike. We saw an American plane for the first time in two and a half years. The Japs loaded us onto a rusty, rotten ship, the *Hokusen Maru*. You wouldn't believe what a crummy-looking ship it was. It wasn't real big, either. The Japs stuffed 1,200 of us aboard, including 200 British and Australians. Their ship had been torpedoed off the coast, and they were the survivors.

"This ship had a stable on one end and a coal bin on the other end. The Japs put half of us in the coal bin and half in the stable. A layer of coal several inches deep covered the coal bin's floor, and this turned out to be a good thing, because it absorbed bodily fluids very well.

"They packed us in there standing shoulder to shoulder. We couldn't move. But before long enough of the men died that we could sit down. The Japs threw the dead men over the side.

"The ship hugged the coastline going north. American subs and planes attacked our convoy. The Japanese didn't mark the ships carrying prisoners of war, so the Americans couldn't tell us apart from combat vessels. We listened to the explosions outside the hull from the darkness of the coal bin. By the time the ship turned away from the Philippines to cross over to Japan, all the ships in the convoy had been sunk except the one I was on. It wasn't for lack of effort, because believe me, they tried to sink us! Some of our people were up on deck cooking rice, and they could see the torpedo wakes heading for us. One torpedo passed by the stern, another passed by the bow, and the third was about to hit amidships when it dove deeper underwater, passed under the ship, and came up on the other side. Torpedoes did that occasionally. It's called porpoising."

I thought about all the twists of fate that had been necessary to allow my conversation with this man sixty years later. Under minutely different circumstances, *microscopically* different, a torpedo would have sunk Louis Read's ship, or a bayonet would have wounded him more seriously, or a bullet that grazed his scalp would have pierced his skull, or the combination of malaria and hepatitis would have overwhelmed him. And I would not be sitting in my dining room talking with Louis Read. Some other man would be looking across the table at me.

"At night, locked in this hold, we could hear the submarines' sonar pings hitting the hull. We had some Navy guys with us, and they knew that sound. They knew what was going on out there. Some of those Navy people were crazy. They called torpedoes fish, and every time they heard that sound, they'd holler, 'Send us a fish, Lord, send us a fish!'

They wanted to get it over with. Some of the men went stark raving mad in there, hearing that noise all night. Several prisoners killed one man because he went crazy and started to get violent. He was climbing on top of people's heads."

"How did they do it?"

"They throttled him.

"A typhoon blew up and bounced that little ship around on the waves, and after a couple days of that, instead of going to Formosa as planned, the Japs diverted to Hong Kong. Everybody got seasick except me and a few others, so I had all the rice I could eat. In Hong Kong they let us climb up the iron ladder one at a time and get some seawater and take a bath.

"The 14th Air Force came over and bombed us, hitting the ship but failing to sink it. After that we set out at midnight and crossed over the southern end of Formosa at a town called Takao. It's called Kaohsiung now. It's only about 600 miles from Manila, but it took us 38 days to travel that distance because of the typhoon and the stop in Hong Kong.

"Before we got off the ship the Japanese brought four Americans on board we'd never seen before and tied them to the mast. They left them there, baking in the sun, and wouldn't let anybody talk to them. Eventually the Japanese turned them loose when we got off the ship, and we found out these guys were off the hell ship *Arisan Maru*. This ship had sailed from Manila two weeks after my ship, carrying 1,800 American prisoners. An American submarine, unaware it carried prisoners, sank it off the Formosa Strait. Nine Americans survived, and these were four of them. The other five, I found out after the war, climbed onto some floating wreckage and were rescued by a Chinese fishing boat. The Chinese helped them get back to the States.

"After two months they loaded us onto another ship and off to Japan we went. I ended up living in the Hosakura prison camp, also known as Sendai 3-B, and working for Mitsubishi in an underground lead-zinc mine in the mountains of northern Japan.

"It was an old World War I mine that had been reopened. It yielded only low-grade ore. We arrived in January to temperatures below zero, snow and ice everywhere. Down in the mine, the temperature stayed at 33 degrees year round. Cold water flowed constantly over everything.

"Above the main shaft this mine had a niche cut in the rock, and in that niche stood an intricately carved pagoda, carved right out of the rock. It was a beautiful thing. Every morning before we went in we had to bow and scrape before the mine's god, who lived in that pagoda, and this was supposed to keep the mine from collapsing. And it worked. That mine never did cave in on us."

"What was it like working down there?"

"I walked along a track about a mile into this mountain and then took one of several lateral tunnels farther in. Then I climbed thirteen flights of rotten ladders up to a very small tunnel in the heart of the mountain, where I worked by myself at the ore face. This tunnel had a little track in it, and at the end of the track was a hole in the floor that led into a chute. I had a cubic-meter ore cart I had to fill, and when I filled it I rolled it to the hole and dumped the ore down into a bigger cart way down below.

"Mitsubishi was tough. They had quotas. My quota was 20 cubic meters a day. I never made anywhere close to that.

A lot of times a draft would come through and blow my carbide lamp out. The Japs had no flint strikers, so we lit our lamp from a fire in the morning and hoped it would stay lit all day. It seldom did. So if it went out we sat there in total darkness and had to wait for a Japanese guard to come by and light it for us. And he'd always take advantage of the opportunity to whack us over the head in the process.

"If we made our quota the Japs rewarded us with a little wooden stick called a chop. We could take that back to camp and turn it in to get an extra rice ball. If we exceeded our quota we got a different kind of chop that entitled us to one Japanese cigarette. A real crappy cigarette."

"But you never made your quota?" I asked.

"Heck no." He laughed harshly. "I wouldn't have made it if I could. The British prisoners in the same mine worked their tails off to get those little rice balls. We Americans figured out pretty quick that you'd use more energy making quota than you'd get out of that rice ball. I don't think a single American prisoner bothered with making quota."

"Tell me more about the guards."

"Our guards were civilians. The Japanese army rented us out to Mitsubishi, which had its own security force. Some of those guys were big and mean looking. They'd whack people over the head for no reason from time to time. As long as you worked or appeared to be working they weren't too bad.

"The most interesting camp I went to was Shinagawa, a prison camp that was supposed to be a hospital. The Japs were battling two big scourges, amoebic dysentery and tuberculosis. They constantly experimented, trying to find cures, and they used us as guinea pigs. They shot us up with a lot of different substances; we almost never knew what.

"The captain in charge of the camp, a doctor named Hisakichi Tokuda, was crazy as a bedbug. He'd do things like shoot soybean juice into the prisoners' spinal columns and they'd die as a result. He did a proctological examination on me, and I had the misfortune to crap on him, and he sent me back to the mine the next day. I would have liked to stay. The food was better there. After the war Tokuda was tried as a war criminal and sentenced to hang. But an American psychiatrist interviewed him and decided he was too crazy to hang, so they never did hang him.

"A Navy admiral visited Shinagawa after the war and liberated the prisoners and said in *Newsweek* magazine it was the filthiest place he'd ever seen. Hell, that was the best Japanese prison camp I was ever in!" He chuckled.

"What was the end of the war like?"

"The Japs had told us they would execute all us prisoners if the Americans invaded Japan. Apparently it was getting pretty close. Huge flights of bombers flew over all the time. The Japs brought in some troops who set up machine guns around the camp and told us they would execute all of us on August 29. There were thousands of American prisoners in Japan, a couple hundred thousand British, Canadian, Dutch, Australian, New Zealanders. There's no doubt in my mind the Japanese would have killed us all.

"I was working in the mine one day and they lined us all up at noon to march us out. That was unusual; the workday was always sunup till sundown. We started thinking, maybe this was the day. We were resigned to it. I knew with certainty I could not survive another winter in those mountains anyway.

"They marched us through a little town, and we saw all these Japanese women standing around and crying. We said, 'Oh, God, here it comes.' All of a sudden the Japanese kids started running alongside us and pulling at our rags, yelling 'The war's over!' in Japanese. We didn't believe it. But it turned out to be true. The Emperor had just given his speech on the radio."

"What was it like the day your camp was liberated?"

"It never was liberated," he said, shaking his head. "We got sick of waiting for somebody to come get us. We had a radio in the camp, and the message we got from Tokyo told us to stay put until somebody came to liberate us. Well on September 13 the war had been over a month, for crying out loud, so we decided, 'The hell with this.' We had some guys who knew how to run a train, so we commandeered a Jap train and went down to Sendai and met up with the Navy there.

"I came back to the States on a Navy hospital ship, USS *Rescue*. Took about ten days to reach San Francisco. By that time I'd eaten so much I'd fattened up. The food was good on that hospital ship. I stayed in hospital two weeks after that, but it took a long while to really recover my health. I had beri beri pretty bad, and I've had peripheral neuropathy ever since the war. Beri beri is a vitamin deficiency disease that kills nerve cells."

"What are your symptoms?" I asked.

"I can't feel anything in my arms and legs. I can cut myself and not know about it until I see the blood. I had a relapse of malaria once in 1947. Haven't had any since then."

Time to ask a pointed question.

"In light of the fact that it once used you for slave labor, what do you think of the Mitsubishi company these days?" I asked, thinking about the sports cars commonly seen on American highways today.

"I don't like any of them," he said firmly, with a hard, cold smile. "I don't think they've changed a damn bit. I don't buy Japanese products if I can help it. Unfortunately sometimes there's not much choice.

"I think their society *appears* to have changed, but if conditions were right and the opportunity presented itself, I think they'd do the same thing over again."

He looked at me with eyes of steel.

"I don't like them. I just don't like them."

The voice was gentle, but the words cut like a knife. I was silent. I come from a politically correct generation not used to such naked expression of one's feelings, but I knew Louis Read's opinions are hardly unique among survivors of the Bataan Death March. Years earlier another death march survivor, Pat Hitchcock of Jackson, Tennessee, had told me, "I still have a lot of anger toward the Japanese. They didn't have to treat us the way they did." And that is really the heart of the matter for the survivors of the march. It didn't have to happen. And though the world has changed a lot, these events are not all that distant in time from us. Thousands of men still walk among us who bear the scars. Who knows how many still walk who inflicted them?

Louis Read in a 1986 photo.

Even if we had money for Christmas gifts,
we couldn't find anything to buy

Shirley Groce Bergeron
Betty Louise Groce Hall
Conroe

"**P**apa was a carpenter, a jack of all trades really," Shirley Bergeron told me, "and he and my brothers built our house on Laura Koppe Road in Houston. Papa built most of the houses in that area, the neighborhood called Shadydale. I don't know if that's still the name. I haven't been out there in years.

"Papa bought a grocery store right across the street. It was really a bad time to go into business. These were hard times for everybody. But it was the only grocery store in our little community.

"We were from a big family, six girls and four boys, and all of the kids had always worked to help out. Four kids were still at home: Betty Lou was fourteen, Susie was twelve, I was nine, and my little brother Rudy was seven. Papa had Betty Lou and Rudy and me work in the store. Susie helped mom at home.

"Papa wanted me in the store because I was always good in math. I worked hard, helping to count the money and check the customers out. Betty Lou and I practically ran

From left to right, Rudy, age 8; Shirley, 10;
Suzie, 13; and Betty Louise, 15.

the store because Papa always had to go search for goods to sell. All the kids in the neighborhood worked at something then, even if it was only a paper route. We didn't think anything about it. Everybody just worked.

"First thing I remember about the war is hearing on the radio Pearl Harbor had been bombed. My brother Lloyd had already joined the service and happened to be at home on leave. He had to go back immediately. He'd been scheduled to get out of the service in January of 1942, just one month later. Of course that was out of the question now."

"What did that day feel like?"

"I remember being scared to death at first. We didn't know whether we'd get bombed, because we didn't know where Pearl Harbor was. It could be right next door for all we knew."

Shirley's sister Betty Louise added, "We had asked if we could stay home from school the next day, but Mom and Pop said we needed to go. Little Rudy asked Pop what we should do if the Japanese came. Pop stared at us for a long time then finally said, 'Do what your teacher tells you to do.' He didn't laugh at us or tell us the Japanese weren't coming here. He may not have *known* for sure.

"I was glad I went to school because the teachers talked about the situation at length, and we listened to President Roosevelt's speech declaring war. We felt safer after that."

"It was a scary time," Shirley said. "We didn't understand war; our generation had never seen it. And can you imagine? Suddenly our brothers and even our fathers were joining up to go to war! It was really sad to see our friends, eighteen-year-old boys, going off to fight."

"How did your lives at home change when the United States entered the war?" I asked.

"Rationing made running the grocery store a challenge," Shirley said. "We had to learn all the OPA rules. OPA was the Office of Price Administration, and it was very strict. We had to be real careful about charging the right prices. They could close us down in a heartbeat if we broke a rule, and they didn't mind doing it back in those days.

"We marked all the goods with both the price and the number of coupons or tokens required to buy it. The government issued coupons, stamps, or tokens to everybody to make purchases. For example, a family might get one sugar stamp a month. Which was great but we couldn't find sugar in the first place! Canned goods were scarce. Shortening, meat, soap, and toilet paper were all hard to get."

"That must have been frustrating," I said.

"Nobody seemed to mind, Stephen, because everybody was in the same boat. Everybody tried to do their part in the war effort; even the kids saved cans, tinfoil, and string. When Rudy could get gum, he used to sit and peel the tinfoil off the gum wrappers. Every once in a while he accumulated a huge ball of tinfoil and string for us to take to a collection center.

"Everybody was involved. Our oldest brothers, J. D. and Snookie, were married and too old to go to the war, but they sure wanted to go. One worked in a shipyard, and one worked in a machine shop that made gun parts."

"You had a brother named Snookie?" I asked.

"His real name is Marion Alfred. The Snookie nickname came from the baby Snookums, a character in the newspaper comic strip "Their Only Child." (It was originally called

"The Newlyweds.") It was a very popular strip, and it became fairly common for mothers to nickname their babies after Snookums. Marion maintains he has hated that nickname all his life, but we don't believe him. We never knew him by anything but that."

"Tell me about some other things you had trouble getting during the rationing," I said.

"Everything," Shirley said. "Shoes, coffee, tires, gasoline. Couldn't get any kind of automotive parts. An old bus from the Pioneer Bus Company made a trip out our way every two hours, and that rickety old bus was literally held together with baling wire. But it made it, and that was our only mode of transportation when we did get to go somewhere."

Betty Lou said, "Laura Koppe Road was just a dirt road out where we lived. The paved section ended three miles away. In January of 1944 the weather got so bad the road became impassable. The Pioneer buses couldn't make it to us through all that mud, so they only came out to the end of the paved surface, and people in our neighborhood who rode the bus to get to work had to walk those extra three miles through the cold and the mud."

"Sometimes it seemed like we worked 24 hours a day," Shirley said. "But on Saturdays, Papa let us go to the movies. Believe it or not, at that time we could go to the movies and spend all day for a quarter."

"You're kidding," I said wistfully, comparing that to the $20 it will cost a couple for a movie date these days.

"Cost a nickel to ride the bus, a nickel to get in the movie, and a nickel to ride the bus back, and that left 10 cents to spend at the concession stand, and that was a lot of money in those days. Enough for candy, sodas."

"Cost a nickel for one movie?"

"No, they always had a double feature and the running serial that was on every week, and a whole bunch of cartoons and then you got to see all the previews, so you could make a whole day out of going to the movies."

"So how long would you be in there?"

"Several hours. The theater would be packed with little kids. And the kids behaved. We just had a good time. "

"What serials did they run between the main features?" I asked.

"Of course we loved the Lone Ranger," Shirley said. "We watched some cowboy serials starring Hoot Gibson. And we always watched the World Path News, which would tell about the war—at least what they were allowed to show, which wasn't much. It wasn't like the Gulf War, which we could watch from home on our TVs. All we knew about the war was what little news we got on the newsreels and the radio. When President Roosevelt spoke on the radio, it was like a church service to us, because we all worshiped him. He was the man, and we trusted everything he said. As a matter of fact my middle name is after Eleanor Roosevelt, because I was born the year he took office, and Papa thought he was the greatest thing since apple pie. I've always admired him and her too, and I'm proud to be named after her."

"What did you do for entertainment besides the movies?"

"There wasn't a whole lot," Shirley said. "We had to work after school. We'd get home from school at 3:30 and sometimes work until 7:30, and then sometimes Papa would say, 'You kids go on and play.' We played a lot of cowboys and Indians. We had a big vacant lot where the kids gathered to play baseball. The girls played too, some of them better than the boys. But I was never very athletic. We just played for fun. Of course girls played with dolls, and the boys would shoot a lot of marbles. The boys had guns carved out of wood with a clothespin and a rubber band made out of an old inner tube if we could find one, and they'd shoot rubber bands at each other. We didn't have structured games like kids have today, and of course we had no television. The radio was the only communication we had with the outside world. We listened to programs at night. *Gangbusters* was about a policeman who fought organized crime. We listened to *Guiding Light* and *Stella Dallas*, soap operas. *Inner Sanctum* was a scary ghost story."

"And did it scare you?"

"Oh yes! It always opened with a creaking door, very creepy. And my dad made us listen to the Grand Ole Opry. He loved that, so we listened to a lot of country and western music."

"Did I hear you right?" I asked, chuckling. "You said he *made* you listen to the Grand Ole Opry."

"That's right," Shirley said, laughing. "We only had one radio. So if we wanted to listen to the radio, sometimes we listened to the Grand Ole Opry whether we wanted to or not. Today I love country and western music, but back then it would not have been my first choice."

"Tell me more about how the kids helped the war effort," I asked.

"When we had sugar to spare we would get together and bake cookies to send to the soldiers overseas. I remember us making lots of fruitcake and boxing it up and sending it over there. We baked a lot of food especially for Lloyd, and some of it he got and some of it he didn't. The mail went by ship and wasn't totally reliable. Could have been sunk for all we knew.

"We took the materials we collected to recycling stations, even used oil. We drove the family car sparingly because if something broke down we couldn't get a part for it. Gasoline was scarce also, and Papa had to use it to hunt down supplies for the store. Being a storeowner entitled him to extra gas coupons, and that helped some.

"To save on fuel, the post office asked everybody in the neighborhood to move their mailboxes down to the grocery store so the postman wouldn't have to drive down all the streets. This way he could just make one stop and deliver all the mail. And everybody did it. They were happy to do it. The grocery store became a gathering place for all the neighbors at 11 o'clock when the postman came. A lot of people had somebody in the war, so they came to see whether they'd get a letter that day. It was a fun time. And people were happy for everybody who got a letter. If you didn't get a letter, maybe you'd get one the next day."

I tried to imagine the reaction if, in this day and age, the post office requested that everyone collect their mail at a central location instead of having it delivered to the front door. I'd hate to be the mailman who had to go around making that request.

"Getting letters from Lloyd was exciting. Papa wasn't a real emotional person, but he would say, 'Here Mom, you

Shirley Bergeron and Betty Louise Hall's parents, Marion William and Bessie Leona Groce, stand in front of their house at 6005 Laura Koppe Road in Houston circa 1941.

read the letter.' We'd all gather around to listen. A lot of times it said nothing more than 'Hello, I'm fine.' He couldn't tell us much. But it was great to hear from him, and Mama would be so happy.

"Sometimes for two or three months we didn't get a letter and then we got five or six all at once. Lloyd wrote them on V-mail, which was a form on a small piece of thin paper. The military censors examined them closely. If they didn't want people to see something, they cut out that section or blacked it out with a marker.

"Did your father ever say anything about Lloyd while he was overseas?"

"Not a lot. But I know he was proud. He would tell people, 'I have a son in the war. We don't know where he is, but he's over there doing his duty.'"

"What was it like for you kids having a brother in the war?"

"Sad," Shirley said. "We were close, and suddenly he was gone and we didn't know where he was. Mama tried to hide her worry from us, but I heard her crying at night. At every meal Papa said the blessing and we prayed for Lloyd and the other boys in the war. 'Heavenly father, we give you our thanks for these and all our blessings, bless this meal and the hands that prepared it.' And then he said, 'Bless Lloyd and take care of him, and bring him home safely to us.'

"Mama always reminded us when we went to bed, 'Don't forget to say your prayers. Remember Lloyd and the other boys, too.'"

Shirley paused. "Both my parents were wonderful. My mom's name was Bessie Leona and my dad's name was

Marion William, but he was Pop to us and Will to everybody else.

"People who had a family member in the war displayed stars in their windows. They had two kinds. People who had someone in the military displayed a blue star. If they had someone who died in the service, they displayed a gold star. It was a little card you placed in your window for people to see. Almost every house had at least one blue star and a lot of them had gold stars."

"And as children, you understood their significance?" I asked.

"Oh, absolutely," Betty Louise said. "We knew in a very real sense that everyone around us was making sacrifices. I remember one year, close to Christmas, Papa got a hind quarter of beef. It was a very rare thing for us to get beef.

"Instead of cutting it up into steaks and roasts like you normally would, Papa cut every bit of that meat up into little chunks of stew meat, so that every one of our customers could get at least a little bit of meat. I closed the store up about 7:30 at night—"

"I'd already gone home because I knew Mama was cooking that stew meat and I couldn't wait. That was a real treat for us," Shirley said.

"It was a cold December night," Betty Louise continued, "but walking home, I stopped in the middle of the street and stared silently at the gold stars in the windows. I knew Mama was cooking that stew meat, and guilt washed over me. I felt so bad because we were enjoying a treat and having such a good time when our boys were over there fighting. I'll never forget that feeling."

"We all had those feelings," Shirley said, getting a lump in her throat. "I remember being so torn up because sometimes when my mother didn't get a letter from Lloyd, I'd wake up in the middle of the night and she'd be crying. I still remember that."

She sniffed and went on. "Some funny things happened too. I remember my customers used to laugh and tease me about working in the store because I could barely see over the counter. I'd stand on a little footstool so I could reach the cash register to check them out. They used to try to fool me. I've always been good at math, worked in accounting all my life. They'd try to give me the wrong amount of money, but I'd catch them every time. They weren't doing it to be mean; it was just a joke. Nobody would ever cheat us. You see, Papa told everybody how smart I was. My brothers and sisters say I was Papa's pet. He bragged to everybody that I could add almost totally in my head. The customers put their groceries up on the counter and I'd write it all down. We didn't have adding machines so I'd add it up, and I'd say, 'That's $2.30.' They'd start pulling out all this change, thinking I wouldn't be able to count it. But I'd stack it all up in rows and see that they'd given me $2.15, and I'd say, 'Mrs. Smith' or 'Mr. Jones, you owe me another 15 cents,' and they'd say, 'Oh gosh, I thought I was gonna fool you, Shirley.'

"And I'd say, 'Nope.' It was funny. Our customers were all good people."

"You operated a cash register by yourself at the age of nine?"

"Yes. It was just part of my job. My daddy told me to do it, so I did."

"What else did you do in the store?"

"Cleaned a lot. We had to do all the price marking; we had a price list and we went exactly by that price list on all the cans. When we could get cold drinks, my brother and I had the job of keeping the soda water box filled up. 'Course back then we didn't have coolers, we just had a big block of ice. Another job I hated was to draw coal oil. A lot of people used coal oil. Oh, that stuff smelled."

"Coal oil?" I asked.

"You know, kerosene for heating and lamps. We drew it from a tank that sat outside the store in a little house by itself. Customers brought little buckets and cans to buy it. A lot of people used it because it was cheaper than electricity. A lot of people didn't even *have* electricity.

"Another thing, you couldn't refuse to sell anybody anything. You weren't supposed to hoard or save goods for particular people. Everybody in the neighborhood knew when Papa drove his old panel truck into town to get supplies, and our regular customers waited for him to get back so they could see what he had. That old truck didn't have a back door, so people on the street could see inside.

"One day two ladies spotted him in downtown Houston when he left the wholesale house, and they saw a case of laundry soap in the back of his truck. They followed him all the way from downtown Houston out to our neighborhood. And each one of them got a box of soap."

"How far is that?"

"I'd say about 35 miles. Sometimes people had to do that sort of thing to get what they needed. We used things very carefully. We grew up learning to drink black coffee with no sugar. Sugar was to be used for baking something for Lloyd."

"Our store shelves were very bare," Betty Louise said. "Papa always searched desperately at every wholesaler he could find for goods to put on those shelves. People in our neighborhood relied a lot on food they canned from their victory gardens. We wouldn't have made it through with our big family if Pop hadn't had the foresight to start raising rabbits and chickens for meat and growing the huge victory garden we all worked in. Thanks to that, we nearly always had chicken on Sunday.

"The older girls couldn't get nylon stockings, so they bought liquid makeup for legs," Shirley said. "It came in different shades just like hose do. The girls painted it on. Hose back in those days had a seam up the back, so the makeup came with a pencil to draw the line up the back of the leg. The stuff worked OK as long as you didn't get caught in the rain! It was funny when that happened because all that leg makeup would just run off. That happened to people a lot.

"Another thing, during the war we couldn't get toothpaste in tubes anymore. I guess it was because the tubes were made of aluminum back then and it was needed for the war effort. Instead, the toothpaste companies like Pepsodent and Colgate came out with tooth powder in a box. You just stuck your wet toothbrush into this box full of powder and then used it to brush your teeth.

"And everybody in the family used the same box...Can you imagine? We didn't think anything of it back then; today it would be a *big* no-no.

"Christmas was pretty sparse. Even if we had money for gifts, we couldn't find anything to buy. I remember Rudy, my little brother, wanted a bicycle so bad. And you couldn't buy a bicycle. One day Papa put him in the truck and said, 'Come on, we're gonna find you a bicycle.' So they went around to all the junkyards, and my daddy finally found enough old parts to put together my little brother's first bicycle. And that's what he got for Christmas."

Again I tried to picture this happening today. It's a difficult scenario to imagine. How many fathers today have the know-how—or the time—to piece together a bicycle out of spare parts? Would a boy of today appreciate the gift, or would he be too embarrassed to let his friends see him with a bicycle built from scrap? Today it's not enough to have the bicycle; it must be brand new, it must be purchased from the right store, and it must be expensive. Most likely, after a few months of use, it will be forgotten and left idle in the garage. But sixty years ago, I'll bet that boy was proud to ride a bicycle built by his own father's hands.

"Our next-door neighbor, Mitzi Fitzhenry, loved all us neighborhood kids and was always so wonderful to us," Shirley said. "I remember she used to call her husband 'Fitz.' She used to take a group of us kids on the bus to the skating rink or to the movies. She even saved her gas coupons and took all of us kids to the San Jacinto River to go swimming.

"On one of these trips, we had to pull over to the side of the road because an Army convoy came through. The soldiers on the trucks saw us kids and started throwing us candy. That was a treat for us; we didn't see candy very often.

"There was just good people back then. Not that there's none today. But we were closer together as a community.

Everybody knew everybody else. I've lived in this apartment complex for almost eleven years now, and I know absolutely nothing about my neighbors. People just don't know each other any more. And it's not just in apartments. In a lot of communities, next-door neighbors don't know each other.

"Back then, we knew what was happening with our neighbors. We knew if somebody needed help; we knew when somebody was sick. I watched Mama and Papa go help people down on their luck many times. When Mama fell ill with colon cancer in 1944 and was in the hospital for several months, the church ladies cooked meals and brought them to us kids, because Papa spent most of his time at the hospital, and it was just us kids at home. That was the way people were back then. When somebody was sick, you cooked a meal to help out. You didn't ask them if they wanted it or needed it, you just did it. It was a wonderful community."

"How do Pearl Harbor and September 11, 2001 compare?" I asked.

Shirley stopped and thought about it. "I remember being nine years old and thinking it was horrible that anybody would want to do this to us. World War II brought out a new side of everybody. Before that we didn't know what war was, and now our boys had to go out and fight for all the good things we enjoyed. But after the initial shock of Pearl Harbor, we children went back to feeling relatively safe and secure. I worried more during the Cuban Missile Crisis when I was grown and married than I did as a kid during World War II, because as you get older, you realize these places aren't as far away as you thought.

"But I will never forget September 11 for as long as I live, because I was sitting here watching the TV, live, as that second plane hit the World Trade Center. I felt utter disbelief that anybody could be so evil as to take out that many innocent people. Even Pearl Harbor, as underhanded as it may have been, was an attack on a military target.

"It's a different world today. Sometimes I think we know too much. We see too much and hear too much. Back then we were more insulated. We found out about battles after they had already happened. Now, we are able to watch an act of incomprehensible evil right as it happens. It's a different world.

"One thing that's the same: the spirit of the American people. They came together in 1941, and they came together in 2001. And it'll always be that way. You can get away with a lot of things, but don't push Americans too far. And I think this time they did push us too far, just like Japan did in 1941.

"It's scary to me that many kids today don't know about Pearl Harbor. It's a shame because young people need to know how they got this freedom everybody takes for granted."

"What do you remember about the last year or so of the war?" I asked.

Betty Lou said, "Early one beautiful morning in June 1944, Mama shook me awake. 'Come in the kitchen and pray with Pop and me,' she said. 'It's D-Day.'

"I didn't know what D-Day meant. It had all been kept so secret. I went into the kitchen where Mom and Pop sat at the table listening to the radio. 'What does it mean, Pop?' I asked.

"He said, 'Our forces are crossing the English Channel and attacking the beaches of France to take it back from the Germans.' The commentators on the radio were telling what little detail they could of the horrible battles being fought.

"Pop turned off the radio, and we bowed our heads and prayed. I'm sure this was going on in homes all over America.

"We opened the store, and all day people walked over and stood around and talked with each other about it, comforting each other and praying in little groups. Churches were full of people all day. Praying, praying, praying. Our church held a special meeting that night. It was packed full of children, young adults, old people, and we all went to our knees to call upon God to help our forces. So many of us had loved ones in the European Theater, and we knew they might be right in the middle of this. So many brave men died that day, but it was the turning point of the war.

"You know," Betty Lou said thoughtfully, "when you consider the equipment and supplies they had to fight with, compared to the high-tech weapons our military has today, you wonder how those boys did it. They had to endure long years of exposure to heat and cold, living on C rations and enduring diseases and every kind of hardship you can imagine. It is amazing to me. I believe God wanted us to win that war. I think He prepared us for it by putting us through the Depression years, teaching us endurance. We were, and still are, a tough, determined people."

"Tell me about Lloyd's homecoming," I said.

"After the Germans surrendered, we all started to wonder how long it would be before Lloyd got to come home,"

Betty Lou said. "Would they make him stay for a long time, or would they let him come home right away? At the time we didn't realize just how many men they had around the world and what a massive undertaking it would be to get them all home.

"Finally in July 1945, Lloyd called us from an airfield in Maine. He had so many points from all the fighting he'd been through, he got to come back to the States pretty quick. In fact, they sent him by plane rather than by ship. He'd just landed and was waiting for his next orders.

"We had no idea where he'd be sent next. The war against Japan was still going on and we worried he might simply be sent over to the Pacific. But Papa said, 'He's been through so much already, I just don't think they'd make him do that.' We knew the military was still taking in large numbers of younger men, so we hoped they wouldn't need Lloyd to go over there.

"They put Lloyd on a train to San Antonio and then on a bus to Houston. He got word to us that his bus should arrive at the downtown Houston station around 9 p.m. Of course in those days you never knew when it would really get there. They'd tell you a time a bus or a train was supposed to show up, but for all you knew it could be several hours after that. Public transportation wasn't as dependable back then.

"My granddaughter Grace asked me recently, 'Why didn't you just drive down to San Antonio and pick him up?'"

Betty Lou chuckled. "Young people don't realize how hard travel was back then. Bus and train were really the only options. Remember, we had rationing. There wasn't enough gasoline for a car trip from Houston to San Antonio, and the tire treads on our car had just about worn through. Rubber was scarce, and so were spare parts.

"My father and I went to meet Lloyd at the station. My mother was too ill to go; she'd had major surgery for colon cancer the year before and was having a long, difficult recovery. The other children didn't go because they were tired from a long day of work. We took the family car, a '38 or '39 Dodge, to downtown Houston. Back then it took about an hour to get there because people didn't drive nearly as fast as they do now. I'm surprised that car made it *that* far, let alone San Antonio, it was in such bad shape.

"When we reached the station around 9 p.m., it was so busy it looked like the middle of day. At least a hundred people were already there, all waiting for servicemen coming home. We couldn't find a place to sit, so we stood and walked around for a long while until we found a bench and sat down together. We couldn't see any sign of Lloyd. Exhausted, I leaned my head back and dozed off.

"Some time after midnight my dad shook me awake and said softly, 'There he is.'

"I opened my eyes and saw him coming, still far away but grinning at us, loaded down with his duffel bag. I screamed his name and jumped up and ran to hug and kiss him. The three of us stood there a long time, celebrating. It was a joyous moment."

"How did he look?" I asked.

"He looked . . . older, and tired. Very tired. I could see in his eyes what he had been through. We rode back home, catching him up on family news. We didn't ask him anything about the war. The newsreels and newspapers told us not to pressure the veterans into talking about what they'd gone through. We were advised to be considerate and let them lead the conversation if they wanted to talk about it."

"Did Lloyd talk about it?"

"No, he didn't talk about it with us for years. For a long time the only person he talked about it with was my husband, John, who'd also been in the war. But on that day we talked only about pleasant things and how good it was to have him back.

"We got home around two in the morning. Mom came down despite her illness, overjoyed. All the children woke up, and we gathered in the living room and talked and laughed and celebrated for hours.

Several of the Groce siblings at a 1987 family reunion. Back row, from left: Robert Rudolph "Rudy", Lloyd Wesley, Shirley Bergeron, Marion Alfred "Snookie." Front row: Melva Hastings, Leona Cecalek, Annie Mae Woodfin Pyburn.

"A few days later Lloyd and I were in a clothing store to buy him some civilian clothes. A salesman came up to help us, and he tried to ask Lloyd something about the war. Lloyd brushed him off, said 'We don't need any help,' and turned his back on him.

"He didn't want to talk about it."

Lloyd Groce eventually did talk about it. His experiences in Europe are detailed in The Courage of Common Men: Texans Remember World War II *(Republic of Texas Press, 2001).*

Shirley Bergeron with brother "Snookie" Groce.

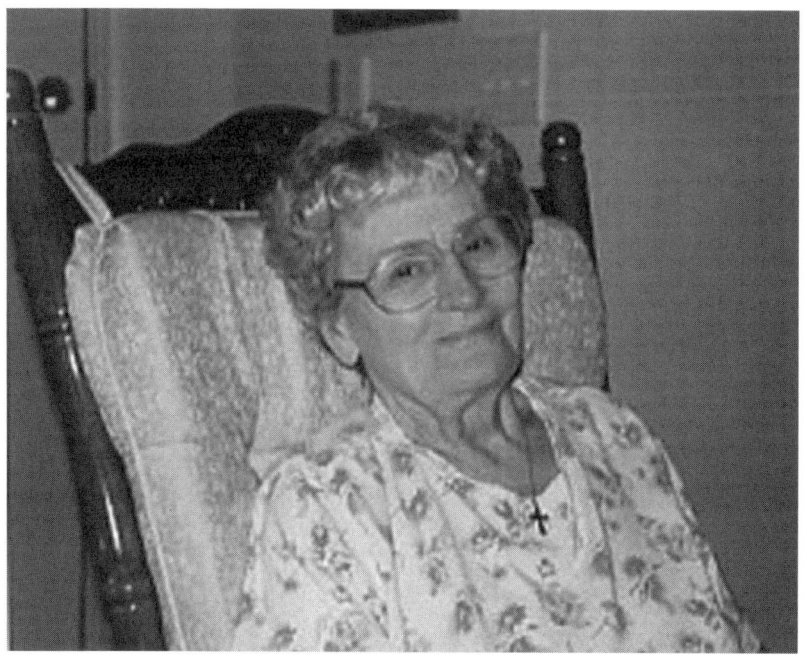

Betty Louise Hall today.

I'm proud to say I liberated a wine cellar

Bernie Travis
Lewisville

Berdyne Travis's wife, Helena, sat in an easy chair nearby and read a novel while he sat with me at his table, flipping through the pages of accumulated newsletters from his veterans association. From time to time a specific memory—a name, a date—taunted him from just out of range and he asked his wife for help. His mouth curled mischievously as he shared a memory he particularly enjoyed.

"I happened to be at home in Ionia, Michigan, the day Pearl Harbor was bombed," he told me. "We were getting ready to go to my older brother's wedding. After we heard about the bombing, I didn't go. I stayed home; I guess you could say I had a lot on my mind. I'd always figured the Army would call sooner or later. Now, there was no question I was going into the service, and soon.

"In January the Army took me to Fort Custer, Michigan. It was 20 degrees below zero. We stayed two or three days, mainly getting needles poked into our arms. Then they sent me to tank training with the 760th Tank Battalion, first in Kentucky, and then at Camp Bowie in Texas."

Bernie Travis as a young man.

He opened a scrapbook, found a picture, and pointed. "Here's a picture of the type of tank we trained in at Camp Bowie."

I didn't recognize it, but it didn't look like much to me. It looked small, unwieldy, and bristly, sort of like a metallic hedgehog. "What kind of tank is that?" I asked dubiously.

He laughed. "The obsolete kind. It was a Grant tank. See, there's no main turret. The big gun here on the side could only traverse a few degrees. As you can see, we were not prepared to go to war.

"After stops for additional training in Georgia and Virginia, we boarded a train to New York to get on a ship and cross over the Atlantic. Up until now we'd only trained in the obsolete tanks. We went to Casablanca without any tanks at all and waited there a month before we finally got our equipment."

"What was your impression of Casablanca?" I asked.

"We never went downtown. But I can tell you this: I've never seen a dirtier place than the area around Casablanca. When we marched through town late at night with no lights because of the blackouts, the place looked beautiful; all the buildings gleamed white in the moonlight. But come morning I'm afraid it didn't look quite so good.

"We got our tanks, trained out in the desert sand, and they finally shipped us over to Naples, Italy. At that time I was the driver of my tank. We arrived in the harbor very late in the afternoon and sat out there through the night. Vesuvius, the volcano right there by Naples, was spewing smoke and fire. That lit up the harbor at night, and we made a good target for the German pilots when they came to bomb. They attacked all along the waterfront. *Bang,*

When the United States entered the war, the 760th Tank Battalion was equipped with the M-3, also known as the Lee and later as the Grant tank. Although it had strong armor, the tank had a major design flaw: its main 75mm gun was positioned at the side where its angle of fire was limited. Fortunately, the M-3 was replaced by the Sherman tank before the 760th went into combat.

bang, bang. Scared me half to death. It was so loud I thought the bombs were hitting our ship. I was down in the stateroom when it started, and I raced up on deck to see what was going on. I saw somebody shoot down one of the German planes.

"Shortly after Christmas our tanks arrived. I was in a 105mm self-propelled howitzer. They were built on the same chassis as a Sherman tank, but they had open tops and no turret."

"Did you have any protection from the elements in those things?"

"None whatsoever. The first place we went was Cassino, with the big abbey on top of the hill that had become a tough German stronghold. We fought around there for a long time. The Germans had tunnels under the hill, and they used the abbey to watch us. The Germans always managed to have the high ground the whole time we fought them in Italy. We were always looking up at them, and they were always looking down at us.

"My assistant driver at that time, fella by the name of Shoop, was the first one of us to get hit. It happened at the first place we stopped, out in the open near some mountains. We knew full well there were Germans up there. But Shoop was off roaming around, looking at the scenery or something, and of course they saw him. And he got it. Took a shrapnel hit. I never saw him again; don't know whether he made it or not.

"We were there quite a while, but we couldn't get them rousted out from there. So we went around them and traveled up north a little ways. Then the Army Air Force bombed the hell out of the abbey. We watched the whole thing. I had to marvel at it, because the pilots synchronized it beautifully. One flight would come in from one direction and drop their bombs, and before they'd hardly gotten out of the target area, another flight came from another direction. It wasn't long before we couldn't even see the abbey. They just flattened it."

"How far away were you?"

"About a mile. All kinds of planes attacked, probably everything we had. I remember seeing P-38s, P-40s up there. Even after that, the Germans still held out in there. But they couldn't get food or supplies so they were no longer a threat to us.

"One night at Cassino I drove the lieutenant's tank because his driver was sick. We always moved at night, the darkest night possible. The lieutenant had 1st platoon, so his tank followed right behind the captain's. It was so dark, we had to follow real close to keep the shape of the tank ahead in sight and not lose it. Most bridges were out, so when we reached a stream we went down one bank, crossed the stream, and came up on the other side. And when we got back on the road we got a faceful of dust. And the exhaust of the tank in front of you would take care of you pretty quick.

"We went along for a while and all of a sudden that black shape started coming right at me. He'd stopped. I pulled back both laterals, but I hit him right in the butt. Wasn't a second before I got rammed in the back, too. But it didn't do any damage.

"The captain gave us instructions to peel off to the left and follow right down through there. He says, 'It's been swept for mines. There's tape marking the path, just follow it.'

"Now I was in the lead. So I drove along those white tapes until we came to the end of them. The lieutenant called the captain and said, 'We've gone through the tapes. What do we do now?'

"The captain said, 'Keep going.' So I started off and before long, *ka-whooom!*

760th Sherman tanks head to battle at Santa Maria Infanta, Italy in May 1944.

760th Sherman tanks after the fighting at Santa Maria Infanta.
Note tank in foreground is missing its tread.

61

"Fortunately it didn't do any major damage. We still had the track on. So we went ahead and moved up into position and executed our firing mission.

"Later we went out to the west coast and moved north to Rome, stopping constantly to conduct firing missions up into the mountains. The German artillery would be embedded on the other side of the mountain, so we couldn't shoot at them directly. The Germans dug tunnels, or rather they'd have the Italians dig tunnels for them, and they'd even have beds in there. We were always amused to see that.

"To get at them over the hills, we used indirect fire. We'd have somebody act as a lookout because we couldn't see what we were shooting at. We'd fire at a high angle so the shell would come down on the other side of the mountain. The observer had to get close enough to see where our shells landed and report back to us. It wasn't always an easy job.

"You know, I was amazed at those 88s the Germans had. When one of those shells passed over your head, you knew nothing could stop it. Once we got hit with a shell. We'd smoked the area in, and we'd stopped and put up a camouflage net. The shell came in, hit the top of the turret of my tank, glanced off and went straight up, and exploded 10 feet above the tank. I was behind the tank digging a foxhole, and after I saw that I dug it a little deeper.

"We took one mountain after another and finally reached Rome. And I'm proud to say," he said with a mischievous smile, "I liberated a wine cellar there." We laughed.

"It was the middle of summer, and those tanks get hot, and the water gets hot in the cans. So everybody started looking for some cold water. My assistant driver and I saw a big round area lined with stone out in a barnyard, and we thought it must be a well. We saw an old man walk up to it and then walk down into the ground. So we followed and looked inside. It was pretty dark down there, but we could see a ladder leading down. We stared down into the hole and discovered there was a door down there.

"Well, this was probably kind of foolish, but we climbed down that ladder and opened that door. It was all lit up in there. I don't know where the man got his electricity. He had huge barrels filled with white wine. The old farmer wasn't too happy to see us, but he drew us each a cup of wine. I didn't drink, but I was thirsty and it was hot, so I tried it. Quite cold, being underground. It was great!

"Then we discovered an outside entrance that led through a clump of brush. We went out that way, returned to the tank, emptied out all the water we had in our five-gallon cans, and went back in carrying those cans. The farmer was even less happy to see us that time! We got that wine and got out of there, but of course by that time the other guys discovered what was going on, and that poor old farmer probably lost all his earnings that year!

"We hung around there for quite a while, and of course we drank a lot more wine than we should have, because it was so cold. This went on until late in the afternoon when the order came to crank her up, we're moving on. So we drove into Rome and drove right past the Coliseum, but we're not to blame for it being the wreck it is.

"We continued on to Lago di Bracciano, a big lake north of Rome. Pulled in there and rested for a few days. The guys went fishing with hand grenades out on the lake in a little boat. That was a dangerous thing to do. This make-shift little boat had water coming up through the bottom. Of course, somebody dropped one of the hand grenades into the bottom of the boat. Everybody dove into the water."

"Was the boat destroyed?"

"Well, it didn't do the boat any good!" he said. "We continued up the west coast. By that time, I had been promoted to tank commander. Each company had one of the 105s, and they'd combine us all together for special operations.

"Heading through the mountains one day, I had a new driver who hadn't been with us very long. Freezing rain had fallen during the night. We traveled down a mountain road, went around a sharp turn, and the driver lost her. The tank skidded sideways, and all we could see was blue sky out there, no guardrails, nothing. That tank was going to go over the edge.

"The rest of the guys were sitting on the back of the tank to keep warm from the engine. I was standing right behind the driver. I saw what was about to happen, and I hollered to the guys in back, 'Jump! Jump!' and I bailed out. I wasn't going with that tank over the side of the mountain, I'll tell you that!

"But the guy got it stopped, teetering right at the edge. It wasn't a sheer drop, but it was steep enough that the tank would start rolling, and you don't stand a chance when that happens. We'd lost a tank that way before, and it killed the tank commander."

"How fast had you been going?" I asked.

"Only about 15 miles an hour, but the momentum of the tank, its weight, and the ice were a deadly combination.

The driver backed it up onto the road, and I relieved him of his driving duty for the rest of the way. We made it to the west coast without further incident. I learned later he was quite a drinker. I don't know if he'd had a drink that day or not.

"My assistant gunner caused me to wear a hearing aid the rest of my life. He was on the lanyard during one of our firing missions, and he pulled the lanyard before I was ready. The gun fired right next to my head, and I went instantly deaf. The medic couldn't do anything for me; he said I probably had a broken eardrum. But some of my hearing came back, and I got along pretty good up until about twenty years ago, when I had to get a hearing aid."

"You must have been pretty angry with him," I said.

He shook his head. "It's just something that happens in war."

He flipped through some papers. "Let's see, where did we go next? These are newsletters from the battalion reunion association I'm looking at. We get them every six months or so. But there's only going to be one more, and then it will be discontinued. Too many of the guys have died. Once that last issue comes out, the association will disband.

"OK, we hit Viareggio, and that's where I got a new tank. The old open-topped tank had a limited elevation on its 105mm howitzer. Sometimes, to get enough elevation on the gun, we'd have to dig under the back of the tracks or run it up onto a log or something. But now we had brand new tanks, Shermans with 360-degree turrets and twin Cadillac engines, beautiful job.

"We took these down to the beach to test-fire the guns because they'd never been fired. We were told not to worry, the beach had been combed for mines and there was tape marking the cleared lanes. Follow the tapes and you'll be fine, they told us.

"So I walked ahead of the tank and led it to the beach. We got through the tapes and I walked off to the right because other tanks were coming up behind mine and we needed to make room for them. My tank sergeant followed me and *ka-whooom!*

"There went my brand new tank. Dirt showered all over me. I had one old guy in the tank, must have been forty-five, riding in the hatch in the turret, and that lid came down on the turret—let's just say he got a Purple Heart."

"Ouch," I said.

"We repaired the tank and moved out that night. Went to Carrara, the town that's famous for its marble. We stopped and rested and prepared for a firing mission near there. A long stone wall stood there, and we pulled up the tanks along it with the gun barrels pointing over the wall. Our infantry fellas were trying to take the church on top of a hill up ahead. We could see them running up the hill, and we fired our guns in support of their attack. The Germans quickly pinpointed the source of the firing—us—and laid down a barrage on us. They had to clear the wall to hit us so they fired behind us, and they hit a little kid, six or seven years old, who was playing back there. Why he was out there I don't know, but when I turned around he was just lying there. I will never forget that.

"When we'd used all our ammunition they brought us more in a half-track and dumped it off behind the tanks. We'd have to cut the tape and pull it off the shells, pull the cap off each shell, and cut out some of the charges. It came with several charges in there, and they'd tell you which charges needed to come out. Maybe you don't want the shell to go up as far, so you cut out several of the charges. You're tailoring the shell to the mission. Sounds like a screwy way to do it, but that was the way we did it. It was quite a job.

"From Carrara on, we just moved forward at full speed. The Germans retreated as fast as they could, and we were right behind them, up until we got to Genoa, and then the war ended.

"You know, all the time I was in B Company, I never drank. The guys would say, 'Aw come on, have a drink.' And I'd say, 'No, I don't drink.' But I told them, 'When the war ends, I'll get drunk with you.'"

"The war ended, so . . ."

"I never saw so many bottles in my life. Anything a guy could want was available. And I tried it all.

"They put me to bed, sat me down, and they told me later I just flopped over backwards. Woke up the next morning and felt great. I saw the boys going to chow and said, 'I better get out there,' and raised up—oh boy. The whole room started to spin. I was on sick call for three days."

Bernie Travis today.

Neil and Toni Gibson
Arlington

Neil Gibson lived on a hilly street in north Arlington, in one of those modern, upscale neighborhoods where the houses are large and beautiful but packed close together, and the yards are small. I drove past neighborhood watch and security system signs until I found the right house. As Gibson led me to his living room, I noticed animal trophies in the corners of my eyes: kudu, sable, leopard, and wolf.

"I was five when the war broke out," Gibson began. "We lived in the country outside Springfield, Missouri. The people all knew each other for a mile around. Here today I don't even know my next-door neighbor, never met him, and I've lived here seven years. But I can still remember the names of the dogs the other families had in the hills around us.

"My father worked for the Cities Service Gas Company as a pipeline engineer. We lived in a company house on a three-acre plot that had all the meter stations for the natural gas pipeline.

"People used to gather across the road at the First and Last Chance General Store. The owner of the store was a World War I veteran and so were a couple of our neighbors.

Neil Gibson visits the beach in Florida with family on Dec. 7, 1941, the day Pearl Harbor was attacked. From left, Neil Gibson, age 5; Neil's mother, Margaret; and Neil's brother, Robert, age 4.

They'd walk up to the store to have lunch every day, and I was old enough to cross the road, so whenever I saw them going in there I'd follow them. I gained admission to the room by emptying out the spittoon for them. I'd sit by the pot-bellied stove and listen while they talked about developments in the outside world. 'Well, they've gone into Poland . . . They've gone into Czechoslovakia. It's gonna come again. Why the hell aren't we over there doing something about it right now?'

"It was pretty evident to these old soldiers what was about to happen. They didn't believe for a minute in Neville Chamberlain's 'peace in our time.' But many people in the United States didn't want us to have anything to do with the problems of the outside world. President Roosevelt thought we should get involved, but the country wasn't ready for it—until the Japanese attacked Pearl Harbor.

"That day was one of the defining moments of my life. I'd gone to Florida with my mother, my grandmother, and my brother, Robert. It had taken us three weeks to get there by car; the interstate system didn't exist then. We stopped every evening and stayed in tourist rooms in somebody's house for the night. We'd visited the Carolinas and then headed south to Florida, all the way down to Miami. None of us suspected anything was about to happen.

"On Sunday, December 7, we had just a few days left of our vacation. We got up, put on our swimsuits, and went to the beach. Even in December it was a very warm day. In those days the streets in Miami Beach only went to about 14th Street. We were staying in the old Olsen Hotel, one of the last before the streets stopped. We had a quarter mile of beach and then it was jungle.

"Nobody else came to the beach that day. To us it seemed warm, I guess everybody else considered it cold. We noticed an Army deuce-and-a-half driving up the street toward us. The truck drove up pretty close to us, and out jumped these Florida National Guard soldiers dressed in World War I-style uniforms with the flat hats, wrapped leggings, and Springfield '03 rifles. They unloaded the truck in a hurry. They didn't kid around. My brother and I just stared while my mother asked them what was happening.

"They said the Japanese had bombed Pearl Harbor, and we were at war. They pointed to a column of smoke visible out on the ocean from just over the horizon and told us a German submarine had torpedoed a Mexican oil freighter.

"My brother and I were just slackjawed. We couldn't imagine it was real. I'd heard the old men in the store talking about this, and now suddenly these soldiers were telling us it had happened.

"A little point of land projected out into the Atlantic from the beach. The soldiers went onto it and dug in a water-cooled machine gun. They dug a horseshoe-shaped trench around the gun and put up barbed wire around it. Then they jacked live rounds into it. They weren't kidding. A dozen men dug foxholes nearby.

"They told my mother and grandmother we had to leave. They expected saboteurs to come ashore from German submarines, and they were setting up to intercept them.

"We went back to the hotel and packed so we could leave in the morning. We looked out the window that night and saw searchlights going every which way, aiming down on the water and up into the sky."

"Were you afraid?" I asked.

"I don't remember being fearful, I remember being totally fascinated. We turned on the radio in the room and listened to all the news.

"It was amazing how quickly everything changed. It went from a balmy Sunday on the beach to World War II just like that. I told you we took three weeks to get to Miami; we took three days to get back home to Springfield.

"My uncle Claire Spears was an FBI agent, and he had told my grandmother and my parents that war was coming, so my grandmother traded her '34 Buick in for a '41 Buick, and my parents bought a '41 Ford. So they got new cars to have during the war just before it became impossible to get them.

"Driving back home, we passed through Pensacola where the big naval base was, and I'm still amazed at how open that base was. We could drive right through it, and the Japs had just bombed Pearl Harbor two days before! We watched PBY seaplanes take off and land. Navy divers wearing flippers swam out and put the wheels on the PBYs so they could roll up on the shore, and they took wheels off other PBYs before they took off. We watched that for about an hour and then looked over at the submarine base a quarter of a mile away. We couldn't drive down there. You cannot imagine all the activity we saw going on at this base. It looked like somebody had stirred up a nest of fire ants. Planes flew everywhere. PBYs in particular flew a lot of submarine patrols up and down the East Coast.

"In Springfield there was more of a sense of shock. The fact that German submarines were operating right off our coast had not been a well-known fact in that part of the country. Communications were so much poorer than they are now; the only thing we saw was newsreels every week at the theater.

"Everybody was used to being calmed by President Roosevelt, because he had essentially turned the Depression around by his force of will. Now people looked to him to do it again. People huddled around radios and listened to him all the time. In fact, a lot of people went out and bought radios right then when the war started so they could get news.

"I remember out in the country the people were very concerned about the fate of their young men who were now flooding the draft boards and Selective Service offices. But as more details gradually got to us of the carnage at Pearl Harbor, a lot of people became very angry.

"The topic on everybody's lips was: 'How can I help? What can we do?' Just like after September 11, 2001. People pulled together. But back then the togetherness lasted much longer.

"Soon the government started to ration things like tires. One of the first things my father did when the war started was to buy a set of tires for the company car, a '37 Chevy, he used to drive around the huge territory he was in charge of."

"I remember very clearly my mother worrying about my father getting drafted. She was tough, but she was worried. He was responsible for the natural gas transmission lines over eastern Oklahoma and western Missouri, and she hoped he would be exempt because of that.

"He came very close to going, and then word came down from the Selective Service board that he'd gotten 1-D.

They deferred him because he had a sensitive job. I never *ever* saw my mother cry, but she did then. I felt her relief deeply.

"My dad got a special gas ration because he drove an average of 200 miles a day covering his territory. The speed limit on Highway 66 was 45 miles per hour, so he had a long day. We lived eight miles out in the country, but my younger brother went to kindergarten in Springfield, Mo., and that caused us a real hardship because of the scarcity of gasoline. I went to grade school about a mile and a half away, so I walked. It wasn't a big deal; I just did it.

"Change came quickly into our lives and didn't stop. The war kept coming and affecting every part of our lives; nothing could get away from it.

"For example, my mother had to get rid of our horses, because all the feed was going to the military, and its price climbed 300 percent. So we sold the horses.

"I remember my grandmother taking me to the bathroom with a flashlight at night, and she would cup her hand over the bulb to dim the light because the neighborhood was having an air raid drill.

"I've got some *Life* magazines from 1943 and '44, and every story and advertisement is somehow war-related. How to make your sheets last longer by taking them off the bed carefully instead of jerking them off. How to make your pantyhose last longer. Jergens Lotion makes your skin softer for when your man comes home from war. Everything was in support of the war.

"That's what made Vietnam such a tragedy; we sent our people in harm's way and then ridiculed them. In World War II if you were driving along and saw a soldier walking down the road, you never thought about it, you pulled over and picked him up. A soldier couldn't walk 20 feet without somebody offering him a ride.

"On the weekends the town filled with soldiers from the nearby Fort Leonard Wood. We'd drive through town and see in a six-block area, a thousand soldiers all over the sidewalks. Families drove down, found two or three soldiers, took them home and fed them, and then brought them back. Those boys ate so many home-cooked meals, they'd almost rather get back to base than have to deal with all the attention. Tremendous patriotism. I've still got the flag we bought right after Pearl Harbor."

I thought about the little flags many people flew—briefly—from their car antennas in the wake of September 11. This sudden bloom of color on the roadways was a grand gesture, but the flags quickly grew tattered and dirty and their numbers dwindled until virtually none remained. But in truth, anyone who displayed one for just two weeks did more than I did; I went to one store looking for one of the little flags to buy, but they had sold out. I never got around to checking at another store. Too busy. Meanwhile, Neil Gibson still has the flag his family bought sixty years ago after Pearl Harbor.

"After she sold the horses, my mom needed something to do, so she volunteered as an Army ambulance driver. They had a local civil patrol set up in case we were attacked and they had to mobilize. The military trained them. At the fairgrounds they gave a demonstration of an infantry squad attacking the end of the football field, showed how they fired and maneuvered, and then there was a 'casualty.' Next thing you know here comes an ambulance driven by Margaret Gibson, and it roared on over and picked the guy up.

"I had a mission in life because I thought I was a combat veteran—I'd seen live ammunition loaded into a machine gun! I took it on myself to collect scrap metal. Word got around in the neighborhood that if you left your aluminum cooking pots out on the back porch, little Buddy Gibson would come steal them, stick them in his Radio Flyer, and take them to be melted down and turned into B-17s.

"Within six months no scrap metal of any kind could be found in the area. Not just because of me but because of everyone helping out. You can't imagine today the unanimity, the total pervasiveness of the war effort."

"What would it take to make that happen again?" I asked.

"It would take either the threat of a foreign invasion or a nuclear detonation. Nothing short of that would do it. We're so lifestyle oriented now, we don't think about anything beyond ourselves.

"At first I sensed people were apprehensive, fearing the unknown, and then as those blue stars in mothers' windows started turning gold, that apprehension transformed into a quiet rage. The carnage was enough to make you numb, particularly in the Pacific. I remember hearing about the island battles, Peleliu, Guadalcanal, Saipan, Tinian... Thousands of Americans dying to take these little scraps of land. Today if we lose one soldier it's a military disaster. I think Americans could still find that old resolution, deep inside. But it would take a major threat to bring it out."

Neil's wife, Toni, arrived home from an outing to a Mexican restaurant with friends. She joined us and listened.

"An interesting thing happened late in the war," Neil continued. "A B-29 lost an engine and made an emergency landing at the Springfield airport. The B-29 was the biggest plane we had, and the Springfield runway was not nearly long enough. The plane went off in the dirt.

"A B-17 carrying a B-29 engine in its bomb bay flew in, and they changed out the bad engine in the B-29 with the new one. There was great speculation in Springfield about whether that B-29 could get out of that airport. They actually took down a row of trees on the east side of the airport, and they stripped everything they could off the plane to lighten it—machine guns, bomb racks, etc., and put it aboard the B-17. They had to wait a day to get enough wind.

"We went out to watch the takeoff, along with three or four thousand other people. People lined up along the streets. Security was light, and we got to walk up and look into the planes."

"That must have been exciting," I said.

"I was just a kid and impressed enough by seeing a B-17 for the first time, but then here was this B-29 that made the B-17 look like a fighter plane."

"Did they manage to get the plane off the ground?"

"The crew taxied the B-29 at least 100 yards off the end of the runway. They only had a pilot, copilot, and crew chief aboard. They didn't even have much fuel, just enough to get to Little Rock. They revved her up good and here they came.

"Dirt and dust and crap flew up behind it, and it was doing 30 mph by the time it hit the runway. The pilot ran it down the runway, and the second the plane felt light he folded the landing gear. He wasn't flying, he just didn't have any landing gear. Then the plane jumped over the trees; if his gear had still been down he would have hit them. The B-17 took off right behind it, and it took the whole runway because it was so loaded down with equipment from the other plane."

"What do you remember about the end of the war?" I asked.

"When we dropped the atomic bomb, Americans understood it was absolutely necessary. We'd had to take Okinawa right before then, and we knew what it would cost us in lives if we had to invade the mainland—even out in the country we knew. In particular, the old guys from World War I understood—if we had to take Okinawa street by street, tree by tree, what would the Japanese mainland be like? If we hadn't done it, we would have needlessly lost hundreds of thousands of our own.

"On VJ Day I was in Ottawa, Kansas, visiting my grandmother. About two o'clock in the afternoon, we heard on the radio the war was over. Japan had surrendered. Steve, I can't begin to describe the emotion that welled up. Just about everybody in Ottawa felt compelled to drive to the courthouse. Two or three thousand people had a huge celebration there on the town square. It wasn't planned, it wasn't run by the government, it was totally spontaneous.

"We went, too. We drove up Eleventh Street to get to Main and passed one house that had a gold star in the window. Everybody else was honking their horns, waving their banners, but in front of this house a lady quietly weeded her flowers. I pointed her out and my grandmother said, 'Yes, we're not going to bother her today.' She didn't look up, she didn't wave, just weeded her flowers while everybody else celebrated.

"She'd lost her son. I didn't know him personally, but I knew who he was. That day was a mixture of joy that it was over and sadness over everyone we'd lost.

"We couldn't park within six blocks of the square. My grandmother had lived in this little country town all her life. She knew everybody and everybody knew her. People slapped each other on the back, danced, it was great. But I still think about the lady out weeding her garden who'd lost her son.

"I didn't personally know anybody killed in the war, but I knew where the homes were that had the gold stars. I knew a lot of kids in school whose uncles were killed. As a nine-year-old, I thought about it a lot: 'I know Jimmy, and his uncle died.' You go to Jimmy's house, and there's a picture of Jimmy's father, and his father's brother, and that's the guy who died. So it was very real. People went to funerals constantly for all the guys coming back in coffins. Even as a young kid, I was touched by the reality and the finality of it. It wasn't just a film.

"People born from 1946 on, people at least ten years younger than I am, don't look at things the way I do. They think people of my generation are a little militant. There's a tremendous gulf, Steve, between those of us old enough to remember how war changed our lives and those of us who aren't. It'll be the same thirty years from now; when twenty-five-year-olds are listening to forty-year-olds, they won't understand what it felt like to watch those planes crash into the World Trade Center. There will be a gulf between those two generations. But September 11 hasn't had a thousandth of the effect on our lives that World War II had."

His wife, Toni, added, "Remember that tremendous wave of patriotism after September 11? Have you noticed that waning some?"

I nodded.

"Back then it didn't wane," she said. "That feeling of patriotism lasted four years. People worked together, everybody pulled in the same direction. And you were proud if somebody in your neighborhood had stars in the window. That sense of pride was sustained through the entire war."

"What else can you remember about the war?" I asked her.

"I was born in 1937, so I don't remember the early part of the war, just the last two or three years," she said. "I grew up in Toledo, Ohio, in a neighborhood where half of the households were immigrant families. All four of my grandparents had come over from Poland. The storekeepers in our neighborhood—butcher shop, grocery store, dry goods store—all spoke Polish to accommodate their customers.

"I vividly remember going to school in the first grade because we had air raid drills. I went to a Catholic school on the second floor above the church, and when we heard the alarm bell ring we had to run down the stairs into the basement. Older children, seventh and eighth graders, were assigned to each one of us to make sure we all got downstairs. When we reached the basement we had to crouch down on the floor and be very still and very quiet. After 10 minutes the teachers would say, 'OK, we can go back upstairs.' We did this quite regularly.

"Being a parochial school we did a lot of praying. We prayed for the war to end, prayed for the people in Europe, prayed for the poor children who were affected by the war."

"Did you ever personally fear the Japanese would come into your neighborhood?"

"Yes, I did a little bit, once I was old enough to fully realize what was going on. We also had air raid drills at night. We lived with my grandmother and her house had no basement, so when the air raid sirens went off she had me sit under the huge old dining room table with its big claw feet. That was my safe place. We had to turn the lights off and pull the shades down until we got the all-clear signal. My parents, Anthony and Genevieve Lewandowski, were never at home during the night drills because they both worked nights, so my grandmother watched over me.

"My parents both worked at a factory making shell casings. Then my father got drafted, and he was all ready to go. He wasn't thrilled about going into the Navy; he would have preferred the Army because he wasn't a good swimmer. But he was ready. Then, just one week before he was due to report in, he received a deferment because of his job as a line supervisor at the plant.

"In 1942 both my parents worked nights seven days a week. In 1943 the factory gave them Sundays off. Then in 1944 the factory went to a five-day week. During the day my mother and my aunts went over to the Red Cross center and packed boxes and rolled bandages to help out.

"That factory is still in business by the way. Acklin Stamping of Toledo, Ohio. It makes refrigerator parts now."

"Were you frightened during these drills, not having your parents there?" I asked.

"Sure, it made it a little more frightening. But I understood why they were working at night; I was old enough to know what was going on."

"What was it like spending the time with your grandmother in the evenings?" I asked.

"There was always something going on in the house. I had one aunt who lived a block away and one aunt who lived two doors down, and they came over to knit and sew and talk and play cards, and some of my twenty-four cousins would always come along, so it was not lonely in the house.

"My grandmother Sophia and I were good buddies. She didn't speak any English, so I grew up bilingual. She and her husband, Jozef Urzykowski, had come to this country right at the turn of the century. She had thirteen grandchildren and was very dismayed that only two of them could speak Polish. Actually I suspect Sophia could speak some English but chose not to. She was proud to live in this country, but she was also very proud to be Polish. She avidly read her Polish newspapers every day.

"She disliked the Germans intensely, but she disliked the Russians even more intensely. She said the Germans were bad but they were more civilized than the Russians. She always referred to the Russians as animals. Ironically she said living under the Russians was better. At the turn of the century, Poland didn't exist as a country; it was divided between Russia and Germany. On the Russian side they were allowed to have their own books and newspapers in Polish, so she could read and write in her own language, while the Germans insisted that everything be done in German in the part of the country they occupied. She said the Russians took a percentage of what their farm produced, but the Germans took much more.

"Poland was prime territory, always being invaded by Germans, Russians, Austrians. Somebody was always eyeing that territory because it had good farmland, good ports. When I visited Warsaw in 1989, a cab driver one day decided he would be our tour guide. He told us, 'You know, I sit in the tavern and I say to my friends, we have a war and the Russians occupy us, we have a war and the Germans occupy us. I think we should declare war against the United States, at least we'd get something good out of it!'

"Sophia told me she and Jozef emigrated because if he stayed, when he turned twenty he would be conscripted into the Russian army, and they would never see him again. The men they took disappeared and never came back.

"He came over first in 1900 and sent for her later. He very much wanted her to come join him, so he kept telling her how absolutely wonderful things were here. So, crossing the Atlantic by ship, she had brought a lot of nice clothes with her, hand-made underthings and such. But as the garments got dirty she simply threw them overboard, because she figured if things were so great in America, Jozef could easily provide her brand new clothes when she got there! Of course he was painting a lovely picture for her so she'd agree to come, but reality wasn't that rosy. He was working in a coal mine when she arrived!" She laughed. "That's one of our favorite family stories."

Young Toni Lewandowski with her grandparents,
Sophia and Joseph Urzykowski, in June 1942.

"And how did she react when she got here?"

"She wasn't thrilled about the loss of all her clothes, but she especially wasn't thrilled to find him working in a coal mine. She worried about his health. Later he worked for a time in a wrought-iron factory, and when things got bad during the Depression he worked as a gravedigger. He did whatever he had to do so they could make ends meet.

"My uncle Adam Klimkiewicz was the neighborhood air raid warden. He volunteered his time. During the drills he patrolled the neighborhood with his big flashlight, wearing his armband, and if he saw lights on in somebody's house, he'd knock on the door and make sure they turned the lights off."

"What did you think of your uncle when you saw him doing this job?"

"I was always very impressed with my uncle. He was a very stern looking man, a stout man with graying hair, who always looked very much in charge. He'd come over to visit for a few minutes and then say, 'Well, I'm gonna go on my rounds,' and he'd set off. He only lived a few doors down from us; in those days families often lived together in the same neighborhood.

"There was a shortage of everything. I remember my mother and my aunts trading ration stamps, 'I'll give you this one if you'll give me that.' We raised a victory garden and so did all our neighbors. Tomatoes, onions, potatoes, and beets took up a big portion of our backyard.

"Of course, butter was nonexistent. So we would go to the store and buy a block of oleo in a pouch, and it came with a capsule full of yellow coloring, and we broke the

Toni Gibson's uncle, Adam Klimkiewicz, served as an air raid warden.

capsule and kneaded the bag, and the white oleo eventually became something that at least *looked* like butter.

"We were very frugal when it came to the car because gas was rationed, and we couldn't get tires. So we walked or used public transportation a lot. Even clothing was in short supply. Nylon was nonexistent. People saved and used everything. When we ate meat we'd save the bones to make soup. If we had food left over, we'd get out the mason jars and put everything up. We wasted nothing.

"Grandmother was always cooking. She made her own noodles. She baked bread. She made pierogi by filling dough with a dry cottage cheese and some onions and she'd drop it into water and boil it to make a large dumpling, then she drained them and browned them up in oleo. That was one of the meatless dinners we had. We had a lot of those. But we had lots of vegetables and lots of soups.

"If she cooked anything that had grease in it, like bacon, she would save that grease to cook with later. Whenever she cleaned a chicken (chickens came with feathers back then) she would save the feathers and use them to make her own pillows. I still have a couple of pillows she made that way.

"These days when you buy a chicken the feet are removed. Back then they weren't. The feet are very yellow and when she made soups, she would put the chicken feet in the water to make the soup yellow and rich looking.

"The supermarket sold pig tails and she would use those for soup stock. If we had vegetables that were getting a little past their time, we'd make vegetable soup out of them. There was none of this 'I'll just pitch this and buy

Toni Gibson's parents, Genevieve and Anthony Lewandowski, celebrating their 50th wedding anniversary in 1984.

something more fresh.' We used everything we had. If milk went sour we used it in baking."

"Were you aware, as a child, of the dead and wounded men coming home from the war?" I asked.

"Oh, yes. A family that had eleven children lived down the street from us, and one of the boys was killed in the war. They brought the body back home. Soldiers carried the casket from their front door down the middle of the street to the church, watched by more than a hundred neighbors who'd gathered on the sidewalks. I remember that day very clearly. The casket had a flag on it. The soldiers wore white gloves. They walked slowly, carrying the casket with the family close behind, and then all the neighbors and church members followed behind them.

"I was awestruck by this sight. Of course I'd seen a lot of this in newsreels, but this was real. It was very sobering. The whole family maintained a solemn composure; I don't remember weeping and wailing of any kind.

"A cousin of mine was among the first from the Toledo area to come back severely wounded in 1942. He spent six to eight months in a hospital and had a plate in his head. He had his picture in the papers because the first wounded were just starting to come back and this was big news.

"Another thing I remember: we had Italian POWs in our city. They were housed in an old school we passed by from time to time. A high fence with barbed wire coiled at the top enclosed the schoolyard. The men hung around in gray uniforms, or rather portions of uniforms. They were always very jovial and waved at us as we drove by. I think they were glad to be out of the war. They didn't seem like they minded being there at all."

"One last question," I said. "What kind of life lessons did you absorb from growing up during World War II?"

"I think mainly self-reliance," Neil said after thinking about it. "Before I was even in grade school, I found out by taking my wagon and going around to pick up scrap metal, that one person can achieve something. One person can make a difference."

Toni Gibson displays a pillow her grandmother made
using the feathers she saved while plucking chickens.

Toni and Neil Gibson today.

*I felt like I was completely
surrounded by bullets*

B. C. Henderson
The Woodlands

"**W**hen the war started I lived on a ranch in Post, Texas," Bertis Clyde Henderson told me. "I had just graduated from high school in Lamesa the previous May. We had ten sections of ranch (a section is one square mile), and about 200 acres of farmland, which we used mainly to grow foodstuffs for the livestock. Life was a daily grind, looking after cattle, long days of chores. In spring and fall we had to do branding. We had to ride the pastures, checking for problems. For example, back then screw worms were a big problem. If a cow got a scratch on it, any slightly open wound, flies would lay eggs in there, and the worms would just about eat a cow up if you didn't catch it early.

"We cut the top off an old cowboy boot and sewed the bottom shut with leather string and fixed a tie at the top. We used it to carry our medicine, tying it to the saddle so it would always be there if we came across a cow that needed treating. We'd rope and throw the cow and put chloroform on the wound to kill the worms. Then we sealed the wound with creosote to keep the flies away and allow the wound to heal.

B. C. Henderson in 1945.

"We had two houses on the ranch so we'd be able to make it home at night after a long day of work and wouldn't have to sleep out."

"Did you like ranching?" I asked.

"It's all I knew growing up. I'd got my fill of it by the time I was grown and decided I didn't want to make that a lifetime. 'Course the war disrupted that anyway. My parents couldn't hire anybody to work the ranch, because all the young men had gone to fight. They had to sell out.

"I didn't hear about Pearl Harbor the day it happened. Anytime I had the opportunity I'd take an odd job, and I was working in town at a frozen food locker plant, cutting meat. A frozen food locker plant was a place where they slaughtered ranchers' and farmers' beeves and rented lockers out to them to hold the meat. Most of those people out in the rural areas didn't have freezers; many didn't even have electricity. We'd quick-freeze the meat, put it in a frozen locker for them, and tag it with a locker number. We'd charge the customers rent on the locker and a fee for processing the beef.

"We didn't have a radio in the plant. I worked a long day and went home late, and we didn't have the radio on at home that night, so I didn't find out then either. I didn't hear about it until the next day.

"The war had already started in Europe, and we'd been sweating it out. We sensed that sooner or later we'd be in it, one way or another. The military had already started drafting twenty-one-year-old men for one year. Most of those who went in under that got sucked up by the war and didn't get out as soon as they had expected.

"A lot of boys who weren't doing too well in high school had dropped out and enlisted. Everybody expected we'd get involved in the war. But we thought it would start in Europe much more than the Pacific.

"Living on a ranch, I had an automatic deferment from the draft because ranching was essential to the food supply, which was essential to the war effort. That lasted a couple of years. But I felt I wasn't doing anybody much good. I felt guilty watching others go into the service while I stayed at home.

"So I notified the draft board I intended to leave the ranch, knowing full well what it meant—it killed my deferment. Just a few months later I got drafted.

"I arrived in Liverpool, England on December 12, 1944. I was offloaded onto a train with other replacements and rode down to Southampton. Didn't know what unit I would be with or where I would be going. In Southampton we waited under a huge shed next to the English Channel for ten hours and then boarded a ship. I saw nothing of England; I was in the country only a day and a half before I crossed the Channel."

"They weren't messing around," I said.

"No, they weren't. We got halfway out into the Channel and then the ship just stopped. For some reason we spent the whole night floating out there in the Channel. In the morning we started up again and landed in France.

"We boarded trains and traveled to an old brick factory near Welkenraedt, Belgium that was being used as a replacement depot, what we called a 'repple depple.' In those places the men sat around with nothing to do, waiting for orders.

"After a couple of days they sent me to the Battle of the Bulge. On December 20, 1994, I arrived at the Elsenborn Ridge and found out I was in B Company, 394th Infantry Regiment, 99th Infantry Division. I didn't know anybody except a few fellas I had trained with, but it turned out I would be sharing my foxhole with a fellow from Texas.

"Trucks drove us into the little town of Elsenborn. It was colder than blazes and the ground was covered with a couple of inches of snow. It snowed a little every night there. Two GIs met us where we offloaded and led us out two miles closer to the Germans. We walked up in the dark to foxholes they'd already dug for us. We'd already been on the front line where we got off the truck, but after walking two more miles, we were *really* on the front line."

"So there were no other Americans in front of you? That was the perimeter?" I asked.

"That's exactly right," he said.

"How did you feel about that?"

"I was scared to death! I knew I was well trained, but there weren't many seasoned men left because the Bulge wiped out so many of them. We were worried because there weren't many people around who knew the score. Of course, before long we would all be baptized by fire.

"One of the men who marched us up there became my foxhole buddy: T. J. Cornett, from Papalote. It's a little community, not even a town any more, just south of Beeville. We got along fine. It made me feel pretty good to be with another Texan."

I just had to look up a place that had a name like Papalote (pronounced papa-*low*-dee), and I learned that in those days, this old railroad town whose name means windmill had a population of around fifty.

"How did the soldiers already there react to the replacements when you arrived?" I asked.

"The more seasoned soldiers were pleased to see us because they badly needed more men. Units were understrength and their lines were very sparse. So they welcomed us with open arms."

"But I've heard a lot about the veteran soldiers resenting the replacements because of their inexperience," I persisted.

"I didn't really see that," he said. "For one thing, there were so few seasoned men, we replacements outnumbered them. The 99th was a brand new division. The ones who'd been there longer than us only had a few days in combat. So even though they were experienced from our perspective, we were not real far behind them. I've heard references to what you describe, but I never saw any of it."

"What did you and Cornett talk about in the foxhole that first night?"

"We talked about where we were from, where we took our training, just idle chat. We had to go and dig more foxholes for future replacements coming up. We always dug foxholes at night because that ridge had very little vegetation, and the Germans were about six hundred yards below us in the woods. In the daylight they could see every move we made."

"How did you dig foxholes in the winter? The ground must have been frozen solid."

"We'd chop a small hole into the frozen ground and stick some TNT in there and detonate it, that's how."

"Did that attract fire from the Germans?" I asked.

"No, they mostly fired at us during the day. They'd hit us with mortar shells, especially if the sun was really bright. In the sunshine, our dark olive drab uniforms stood out like a sore thumb. They could see us but we couldn't see them. So we stayed in the foxholes during the day and ran patrols and dug foxholes at night."

"How long were you on the ridge?" I asked.

"Six weeks. Six weeks of beating back German attacks, dodging mortar shells, and running patrols. As the day passed we sat there and listened as they lobbed shells at us. We could hear their big artillery going overhead and the buzz bombs going by. They made a putt-putt sound. I've heard people say it sounded like a Model T Ford. We couldn't see them; they were above the clouds. And we couldn't see the Germans at all. More often than not it was very cloudy or snowing."

"How accurate was the German fire?"

"Their mortar fire was deadly accurate. We just hunkered down when it started coming in. During the night we gathered up everything we could find, logs, boxes, etc. to cover up our foxholes and protect us from shrapnel. It would take a direct hit for a mortar to get us when we were in the foxholes. But a lot of people got hurt or killed by mortars because they were up and about when the mortar shells hit, and the shrapnel got them. People just had to get out of the foxholes sometimes, to get ammo for the night, rations, what have you. So people got hurt."

"What effect on morale did sitting in a foxhole all day have on you?"

"Sitting there doing nothing gave us too much time to think and wonder what lies ahead. Before long those thoughts creep into your mind: 'I wonder whether I'll ever get out of this?' The longer we sat there the more doubt we had that we would ever get out. It was just too much time to think."

"What did you do to try to pass the time?"

"Of course we'd write letters and read mail when we got it. On the ridge we'd get mail every few days pretty reliably because we were stationary, but after that when we were on the move, we didn't get it nearly as often. Sitting there got pretty boring. We ran out of things to talk about pretty quick, but we tried to keep some type of conversation going, because the last thing you wanted to do was just sit there and get numb. Of course we got as much sleep as we could during the day because at night we worked or went on patrols. We hated patrols."

"Tell me about the worst patrol you ever went on."

"On January 15, 1945, B Company assembled thirty men and one officer from all the platoons. The company was so understrength, putting this patrol together nearly depleted it. A lot of us were so new we didn't know each other's names.

"At around four in the morning we headed toward the woods in front of the ridge to try to determine the strength of the German forces down there. According to the plan, we would wait at the edge of the woods and wait for our own planes to show up just before daylight and strafe the German positions.

"We waited. The planes didn't come. The sun rose and they still didn't come. There we were, totally exposed, lying in the snow outside the woods. Our officer ordered us to move into the trees. The minute we moved, the Germans opened fire on us.

"As soon as we got into the trees we heard the roar of aircraft engines. Our own P-51s made their belated entrance, swooped down, and strafed the hell out of us. We were getting hit from in front and above.

"About 100 yards inside the treeline, a German machine gun nest pinned us down. The man on our light machine gun got hit. Some men pulled him back and I tried to take his place at the machine gun, but as soon as I moved into position in the impression his body had made in the snow, I took a bullet in the arm.

"It felt like a sledgehammer. This bullet ricocheted off a tree, entered my shoulder and burrowed down the arm toward the elbow, where it stopped. My entire arm went numb.

"Then Cornett took our bazooka, managed to get into a good firing position, and took out that machine gun nest. He got a Silver Star for that.

"We had a lot of casualties and we were low on ammo, so we got the order to withdraw. In order to do that, we had to make our way back up the slope to the ridge in broad daylight. I mentioned before, there was very little vegetation on that ridge to use as cover, and to make matters worse we had to get through minefields and knee-deep snow.

"We spread out to make smaller targets. I had been ordered to go ahead of the main group because I was wounded. I tucked my wounded arm into the front of my jacket and ran as far and as fast as I could. Bullets kicked up snow around me. The deep snow quickly exhausted me. I fell flat on my face and lay there, perfectly still.

"The Germans stopped firing at me, thinking I was dead. I rested there a while and when I felt ready, I jumped up and ran. More bullets hit the snow around me. I had to stop to catch my breath several times, and each time the Germans stopped shooting at me. I finally made it back to our front line."

"How many of the thirty made it back?" I asked.

"Thirteen. And nine of the thirteen were wounded. Jeeps carried us to the aid station in Elsenborn. I rode in the same jeep with a Sgt. Doebler who'd stepped on a mine. Half of his foot was dangling, held in place only by a small strip of boot leather."

"How long were you out of action?"

"They removed the bullet, put my arm in a sling, and sent me back to my foxhole. The wound wasn't serious enough to put me out of commission. I still have that bullet. It's mounted next to my Purple Heart.

"On January 30 at three in the morning we left the Elsenborn Ridge to clear out the eastern edge of the Monschau Forest, southeast of the ridge. We spent three days and nights without rest, struggling through waist-deep snow. That forest was so dense and dark we could barely see anything in the middle of the day. The snow came up to the bottom branches of the trees, so you can imagine the difficulty of moving around in there. The Germans resisted fiercely; after 15 hours we'd only advanced 500 yards. We ran into a bunch of boobytraps and anti-personnel mines. Lost several people to those.

"Wheeled vehicles couldn't get into the forest because of the waist-deep snow and heavy underbrush. To evacuate our casualties, we had to carry them by ski-sled out to a Weasel, a small tracked vehicle, which carried them farther out to a litter jeep, which carried them out to an ambulance.

"One night I led three men on a patrol. I couldn't see my hand in front of my face. To keep from getting separated, I tied a rope around my waist and told the other men to hold on. We crawled most of the way to get under the tree branches. We made it to a little clearing and stood up, and I stumbled over a trip wire. A heck of a racket shattered the stillness and we ducked, expecting an explosion. But the wire was only connected to tin cans filled with rocks. If it had been a booby trap I'd be dead.

"We lay still waiting for Germans to attack, alerted by the noise, but none did. We started moving again and I fell into a big hole. The other three men, following the rope, fell in with me. I was alarmed at first because I didn't know what we had fallen into, but it turned out to be just a hole, a hole large enough to swallow a tank.

"I lost my helmet during the fall, and we crawled around trying to find it but couldn't. A GI felt naked without his helmet. Sometimes during combat a soldier felt like he could crawl completely under that helmet. After a while we gave up searching and made our way back, with me wearing nothing on my head but a knit cap.

"We had only a poncho to keep us dry and warm that whole three days, and we ate only the K-rations we carried with us. It wore us out. But we rooted the Germans out of there.

"After the three days we stumbled back to the ridge, slipping on ice and too numb to care about anything. The ground had begun to thaw a little bit, and the foxholes had water in them. So we bunked down on the wet ground that night. The next day they pulled us back to the rear for a little R&R. They put us to work building roads! So there wasn't much rest. But it was considered R&R because we weren't being shot at, you see."

"Were you glad to be building roads, then?"

"Oh yeah, because we weren't getting shot at! It was a good break from being on the front line. I got a 24-hour pass to go to Brussels and take a bath and sleep in a bed and put on some clean clothes. It had been a month since my last shower. It was nice to get clean. But then as you go back, you start worrying about the fact that you've been away from the fighting for so long, and it's like starting over. You have to steel yourself all over again.

"We went back to the front, pushed off, and started to cross the Cologne Plain in hot pursuit of the retreating Jerries. We did a lot of fighting on the run. Gosh, if we happened to find an old bicycle, we'd hop on it and pedal toward the Germans.

"We trekked all the way from Aachen to Cologne, losing quite a few men on the way. The retreating Germans repeatedly stopped and turned to fight us, harass us. Their artillery killed our company commander. He had taken cover in an old crater where an artillery shell had hit earlier, and some shrapnel got him while he was in there.

"A few times it got down to house-to-house fighting. We'd go door-to-door, kick in the door, throw in a hand grenade, and after it exploded we'd go in firing. We lost a lot of people that way. One time there was a fellow from Texas, I can't remember his name, every time we'd get a break and sit down, he'd sing 'Don't Fence Me In.' He was down on his knees crawling by the buildings to see if anybody was down in the basement. He crawled past a building where a Jerry was hiding down there, and that Jerry shot him and cut his throat.

"Crossing the plain was just a constant grind day and night, totally wearing ourselves into the ground. Village fighting got tedious. One village started to look like another. We'd clear out one and move on to the next.

"We got within sight of Cologne, right up at the river. We could see the spires of the cathedral. Our commanders were trying to figure out how we were gonna get across. Then all of a sudden they loaded us onto trucks and rushed us down the river to Remagen. The Ludendorff Bridge had been captured, and we were ordered to get across and help establish a bridgehead. We endured a rough ride over the hills at high speed, packed into those trucks like sardines and bouncing and bumping each other.

"The 9th Armored Division had managed to capture the bridge intact, despite German attempts to blow it up. This was a major setback for the Germans; it was the only bridge still standing over the Rhine. Now we had to get large numbers of troops across it, fast, before we lost our chance.

"That was a very, very scary situation. We waited until night to cross, hiding in a basement to avoid the shelling. The Germans had the ramp leading onto the bridge zeroed in. They threw all sizes of artillery—mortars, 88s—everything they had at us from positions behind a mountain across the river. Shells landed near the foot of the bridge every 30 seconds. Many men died right there.

"As we prepared to cross I crouched down behind a jeep and trailer for protection. A shell hit nearby and a fist-sized piece of shrapnel punched through the trailer just above my back.

"The bridge was too damaged for trucks to cross, so we had to walk it. We lined up single file on either side of the street and ran up the ramp with orders not to stop for anybody or anything, not even to help the wounded men lying around calling for help. We had to step over them. I'll never forget hearing them cry out, 'Medic! Medic! I'm bleeding to death!'

"As we entered the bridge, the Germans fired at us from the other side of the river. They gave us fits with all that small arms fire. Shrapnel flew everywhere. We crossed the bridge in pitch dark."

"How did you see where you were going?"

"When shells exploded, they lit up the skyline and gave us a brief outline of the bridge. That was the only way we could see. The bridge floor had holes in it large enough for a tank to fall through. Fifty feet below us, the Rhine River rushed by, so we had to concentrate on avoiding the holes as well as dodging the enemy fire. We figured with every step one of those shells was gonna get us. We were shooting from the hip, more or less, because we couldn't see anything.

"Bullets bounced off the beams around me, ricocheting everywhere. I felt like I was completely surrounded by bullets. I still remember them zinging past my ears."

"How did you manage to avoid the holes?"

"It was really hard to see them, so we hugged the framework on the sides of the bridge. The holes were more toward the center. The framework also gave us a little protection against enemy fire. The water below was very cold; you couldn't live very long in it. If the fall didn't get you, the cold water would."

"How long did it take to get across?"

"It was four or five hundred yards across the bridge and ramp. Seemed like it took a couple of hours. Sometimes it seemed like I was the only one there and all the Germans were shooting at me.

"Partway across, I felt like I couldn't take another step. I started to tell myself it wasn't worth it because even if I reached the other side, the Jerries were waiting there to gun me down. But I managed to pull it back together and tell myself, 'I'll get them before they get me.' And I kept going.

"When we got across we checked out the railroad tunnel on the other side to make sure there weren't any Germans shooting at us from in there. There weren't any living ones. But we found a large number of dead ones sprawled across the tracks.

"We moved up the river and dug foxholes and set up a perimeter near Linz. We stayed there a couple of days and ate K-rations that a Piper Cub dropped to us.

"The service companies started gathering up dead GIs and piling them up by the truckload. I saw a truck roll by full of our own men, stacked like cordwood. That was a gruesome sight. Of course we'd already stepped over a bunch of them on the way here, but to see so many of them

B. C. Henderson poses in Nuremberg in 1945.

stacked up like that kind of knocked us to our knees. It was hard to deal with, but we went on about our business.

"The next day we headed into the mountains to clear them out. Fighting in the mountains exhausted us. Always going up and down, carrying a full load of ammo. We couldn't dig foxholes in the rocky ground, so we just dug little slits we could lie in, just deep enough to cover most of our body.

"A fellow named Heim in our platoon got hit right between the eyes in the helmet. The bullet circled the inside, cut his helmet liner and scratched his head, just a flesh wound, and came out at the very back of his helmet.

As soon as the fighting died down he took it off and we looked at it, and if you didn't know better, you'd think that bullet had gone straight through his head. At first it scared the heck out of him and then it was kind of funny.

"I'd gone through basic training with this guy Heim, who came from a logging family somewhere up in the northern states. His family sent him some bright red high top socks, boot socks. He swore the Germans could see those socks in the dark, and that's why he got shot at, so he threw them away.

"Fighting began to slack. We turned east and had some fairly light fighting for a while. We didn't know it at the time but a couple of German armies had surrounded the Ruhr Valley and formed the Ruhr Pocket. We headed up there to join the fight.

"Just before we got to the Ruhr Pocket, we liberated a POW camp at Hadamar full of starved prisoners, nothing but skin and bones. Walking skeletons. They were Russian, Polish, and British mainly. A few Americans. We found some sealed up in boxcars and some already dead. The Germans were trying to dispose of the prisoners before we got there, but we got there soon enough to stop it—for the most part. The worst thing I saw was two starving prisoners, so weak they couldn't stand up, but they were trying to fight each other over a dead cat to eat. That really got to me.

"It took us almost two weeks to finish off the Ruhr Pocket. We took literally thousands of German prisoners. The Germans would put up a good fight and then when they knew all was lost they'd surrender as a unit, so we'd take huge groups of prisoners all at once. Finally, we closed the pocket on April 17.

"On April 30 we liberated another prison camp at Moosburg, a subcamp of the famous concentration camp at Dachau, near Munich. This camp had some American men who'd been captured in the Battle of the Bulge. It was great to be able to set these people free."

"What was your reaction when you saw the camps?"

"Disbelief and horror. We couldn't believe what one human could do to another human. Fortunately, the war ended pretty soon after that."

"How soon did you get to go home?"

"Almost a year after the war ended. My dad had been bedridden for a long time because of a heart attack, and he'd just gotten out of bed when I got home. It was a very happy reunion. My mom hugged my neck and wanted to feed me, bake me pies, cook me anything I wanted, anything she could do to make me happy. It would have been perfect if my brother Jim had made it back too, but he was killed in November 1945. He was electrocuted while working on a high-power line in Korea."

B. C. Henderson today.

We felt we really had a part
in the outcome of the war

Marie Hobbs – Arlington
Dell Nail – Arlington
Freda Holt – Austin
Rubye Marston – Arlington
Dorothy Garmon – Manor
Daphne Moody – Elgin

I crossed a small bridge over a stream and drove down curvy roads into a pleasant, well-kept neighborhood in Arlington. I found the home of Marie Hobbs, knocked on the door, and was let inside. Six pairs of friendly, curious eyes examined me.

"I've been looking all over for you ladies," I said.

No book like this would be complete without the story of Rosie the Riveter. With few men left to perform jobs vital to the war effort, women stepped up in droves, leaving their homes to help out—not just by riveting, but by performing countless tasks that had traditionally been part of the male domain. It may not seem like a big deal today, but back then it was a big change for the country.

The Thompson sisters take part in a patriotic radio show broadcast from beneath the bomb bay of a partially constructed B-24. From left, Jewell Stevenson, Rubye Marsden, Freda Holt, Marie Hobbs, Daphne Moody, and Dell Nail.

At first I had trouble finding a Rosie to interview, which surprised me because Fort Worth was home to the huge Consolidated plant that built B-24 Liberators. But nobody I contacted seemed to know any women who worked in the factories during the war. Even turning to certain organizations one would naturally turn to for such information proved fruitless. I started to despair of finding anyone, telling myself too much time had passed, they were all gone. It was a stark reminder that we need to preserve these stories while we have the chance.

But then I stumbled across a treasure.

I found a newspaper article, several years old, about the seven Thompson sisters, who all went to work during the war—six of them at the Fort Worth plant. If I could find them, I would go from having zero to having several just like that. By now the sisters were scattered across the state, but I tracked one down. Dell Nail told me the sisters get together often, and she invited me to come visit with them.

We spent a few minutes on introductions and small talk. Dorothy Garmon, Marie Hobbs, Freda Holt, Rubye Marston, Daphne Moody, and Dell Nail were all there. The oldest sister, Jewel, passed away in 1949. Marie, Freda, Rubye, Daphne, Dell, and Jewel had all worked at Consolidated during the war, and Dorothy worked at Southwestern Bell.

We pulled up some extra chairs into the living room and put them in front of the couches to make a circle. We sat down and I placed my tape recorder on a seat in the center. The ladies watched me expectantly.

"What do you ladies remember about the day the war started?" I asked for starters.

I was met by groans, cackles, shaking heads, and rolling eyes. The ladies all spoke at once. "You want us to remember that far back? How am I supposed to remember that? I can't remember what I was doing last week."

Uh-oh, I thought, but I don't give up easily. "Let's try one person at a time," I suggested.

Dorothy went first. "My husband, Giles, and I went to downtown Fort Worth to watch a movie. After we heard Pearl Harbor had been bombed, we rushed to Marie's house

A real sister team, these five women workers at Consolidated Vultee's Fort Worth plant. Shown in one of the B-24 bombers they help build, left to right, Mrs. Daphne Moody, Mrs. Marie Hobbs, Mrs. Dell Nail, Miss Freda Thompson and Mrs. Jewell Stephenson. Two other daughters expect to qualify for jobs at the plant, making a seven-sister team.

GLADEWATER MAGNOLIA MAN HAS SEVEN DAUGHTERS IN WAR WORK

Fred Thompson, the father, has been a Pipe Line Engineer for the Company for eighteen years. The family home is at Gladewater, Texas.

Six of the girls are married and their husbands are either in the armed services or are doing essential war work.

Five of the sisters are working at the Consolidated Vultee plant at Fort Worth. They are: Miss Freda Thompson, Mrs. Dell Nail, Mrs. Daphne Moody, Mrs. Marie Hobbs and Mrs. Jewell Stephenson.

The two other sisters are Mrs. Rubye Marston and Mrs. Dorothy Garmon. Rubye is in training at Fort Worth for

Consolidated work, while Dorothy, by the time the Magnolia News is issued, will be with her.

Parents of the seven-sister war-work team have ten children in all, the three others being boys, Fred, Jr., Wray and Lynn, all in school at Gladewater.

Checking up on the six husbands, Nail is with an ordnance plant at Marshall, Moody has been overseas eleven months, Marston is at the Corpus Christi ship-yards, Hobbs drives a truck for essential construction work, Stephenson is at Consolidated, Garmon is with another Fort Worth aircraft plant.

The Magnolia Oil Company, employer of the Thompson sisters' father, ran this article and photo of the sisters in its employee magazine.

on Avenue I to tell Marie and her husband, Bay. The four of us spent the rest of the day talking about it and what it meant."

"That sounds about right," Marie said. "They were always hanging around at my place."

"What did you talk about?" I asked.

"Well, we didn't know much about Pearl Harbor," Marie said. "We started wondering, should we try to go to work to help out?"

"I had never worked before," Dorothy said. "But I got a job as a long-distance switchboard operator for Southwestern Bell. It was considered vital work for the war effort. Of course, the telephone system worked a lot differently in those days. We sat in front of a wooden panel full of wires, and we had to plug in the cords where the lights were lighting up.

"Southwestern Bell taught us that we were there to help people. In those days we did something that would never happen today. Not everybody owned a telephone, so if somebody called for Mr. Smith who didn't have a phone, we could call Mr. Jones across the street from him and ask him to go get his neighbor on the phone so we could connect him with the caller.

"And if we happened to know where somebody was at the time they got a call, we'd send the call to where they were rather than to their home phone number. It was a small town, see, so we knew who was where.

"But sometimes that led to unfortunate consequences. One time a woman called her husband, and I knew where he was because I'd just put a call through for him a few minutes earlier. So I connected her to that number, and the woman he was with answered the phone. There was a big to-do about it." She shook her head ruefully. "I was just trying to help."

When it was Rubye's turn, she thought hard for a moment and said, "I'm sorry, I can't remember that day. I'm trying, but everything just disintegrates." The sisters all chuckled.

We continued around the circle. Daphne said, "I was fifteen and still living with my parents in Gladewater when Pearl Harbor happened. Our father worked for the Magnolia Oil Company.

"My future husband, Ben, was already in the military; he'd enlisted the year before because they were told they would get out after one year. Once Pearl Harbor happened, they could forget about that. He came home on leave for a week and on January 2, 1942, we got married. It was probably pretty foolish getting married at the age of fifteen, but it seemed like the right thing to do at the time. We didn't know when he'd be coming back, if ever."

"I was single and I was training for defense work in Gladewater," Freda said. "They set up a community training center there where we could learn the skills needed to work in a plant. I came to Consolidated here in Fort Worth, and they set up a fake factory in the Will Rogers Coliseum with machines for us to train on. I trained to work in the machine shop area. That's where we measured the parts to make sure they were precisely right, and if they weren't, we would grind them down or whatever we had to do to get them right."

"What was it like when you first went to find work?" I asked.

"I remember when I went to qualify to work at the Consolidated plant," Daphne said, "there was a girl a couple years older than me. I was sixteen and she was eighteen. She was one of those giggly kind of girls, the ones who can't say anything without giggling. They interviewed her and then they interviewed me, and I lied about my age because you had to be eighteen to work there. They decided this other girl couldn't be as old as she said she was, because she wasn't mature enough. So she didn't get

A pay stub issued to Daphne Moody,
showing a week's net pay of $22.99.

hired. But they hired me, even though I was the one who was lying about my age.

"You know," Daphne said, "I had never even learned to ride a bicycle; we couldn't afford one when I was growing up. I'd also never driven a car. In fact none of us girls learned to drive until after we got married. I guess our parents hadn't considered it important that we learn to drive."

"Let me get this straight," I said. "You were working in a B-24 factory before you knew how to ride a bicycle or drive a car?"

"That's right."

"Were you nervous at all, the first day you went to work?" I asked her.

"I didn't have enough sense to be nervous," Daphne said. "At that age, you have all the confidence in the world. You know everything. And I knew what I was supposed to do. I didn't have any problems on the job."

"How did men take to the idea of women leaving the home and going to work?" I asked.

"Most of the men were proud," Dorothy said.

"We felt we really had a part in the outcome of the war," Marie said.

"That's right," Daphne said. "We felt like it was absolutely necessary that we do this. Everybody was trying to do something for the war effort. And with my husband fighting overseas, helping the war effort became my primary concern."

"How did you get to work?" I asked.

Marie said, "At 5 a.m. we caught a bus to ride to work. It was actually a cattle trailer."

"I drove," Dell said indignantly.

"You was uptown," Marie retorted. The sisters laughed.

"How long was your shift?" I asked.

"We worked eight hours and had half an hour for lunch," Daphne said. "I was working up on the mezzanine in receiving, and at lunch I usually went downstairs on the floor where my sisters were, and we'd sit down to eat on the floor, lined up against the wall under the mezzanine. There was no other place to sit. The plant didn't have a cafeteria. We brought our own lunch.

"We worked until 3:30 p.m. and went home. We'd get our clothes ready for the next day, and we'd fix up our hair for the next day, whatever we were going to do about it, and we'd go to bed because we had to get up so early. We'd be in bed by 9 p.m."

"Did the job tire you out?"

"We were young and energetic. We didn't tire that easily," Daphne said. "I felt like I could work a 24-hour shift if need be. Except when I started donating blood. They asked us to donate as much blood as we could, and Rubye and I donated it as often as the nurses said we could come back. But I gave too much, and I got anemic. The doctor told me not to go there anymore."

"How many people worked at the plant?" I asked.

I got shrugs and blank looks. "Lots. Thousands, certainly," someone said. "That plant was the biggest place we'd ever seen."

"Did you doubt at any time that we would win the war?"

All the sisters shook their heads firmly. "No, never doubted it for a minute," Marie said.

I asked what kind of jobs they performed at the plant. Marie and Rubye were riveters. Daphne sharpened drill bits. Dell built control surfaces, and Freda worked in the machine shop.

"We were just dumb kids, you know," Marie said. "I put a rivet into a lady's knee."

The sisters laughed. "What!?" I asked.

"The two of us were working together; I was inside the plane and she was outside. I was driving rivets outward and she was bucking the piece of metal I was riveting, that is, holding it into place so it wouldn't warp while I riveted. We had a system of communicating by knocking on the metal to tell the other person 'OK, continue,' and so on.

"Well, I accidentally sent a rivet in too deep and it went all the way through the outer skin. I waited to hear her knock and didn't hear anything, so I went out to check on her. I saw a trail of blood leading toward the infirmary."

"What did you think?" I asked.

"I had no idea where I'd hit her with that rivet. I hurried over to the infirmary to see how badly she was hurt. It turned out she had rested her knee against the skin of the aircraft right at the point where I was riveting, and when I drove that rivet through the metal I riveted her in the knee. She was back at work wearing a bandage the same day, but I'm sure that taught her not to press her knee against the plane. You're not supposed to do that."

Daphne showed me a small booklet that said Magnolia News. "Our father, Fred Thompson, was recognized in the Magnolia Oil Company's employee publication for having so many daughters helping the war effort," she said.

The inside pages were black and white but the cover was printed with blue and red ink and showed an American flag blazing over a map of Texas and surrounding states. She flipped it over to the back cover and there, printed in blue, was a cheery image of five young women peering out from the waist gunner's position in the side of a B-24. She showed me another photo of all six of the sisters who worked at the plant taking part in a radio program, reading scripts around a microphone beneath the bomb bay of a partially completed B-24. They appeared to be having a good time, glancing at each other and smiling as they read their lines.

"They told us precisely what to say on the air," Daphne said. "There was no ad-libbing, we just read from the script."

"I didn't spend the whole war at the plant," Rubye said. "I went into the WAVEs and served in the hospital corps. They assigned me first to Hunter College in New York and then to Corpus Christi."

"Why did you decide to join up?" I asked.

"I saw so many other people going into the service, I thought maybe I should too," she said. "It was a way to be helpful. I really enjoyed my service."

"What was it like when the war ended?" I asked.

"It was hard after the war," Dorothy said. "Everything was chaotic. Giles was a prisoner of war; he'd been captured by the Germans during the Battle of the Bulge. After the war ended and he came back, it took us a couple of years to get settled down and back to normal. We couldn't get appliances for the house. There wasn't enough of anything. We couldn't just go buy things. And Giles had to

From left, Rubye Marston, Daphne Moody, Dorothy Garmon, Marie Hobbs, Dell Nail, and Freda Holt.

recover his health. He weighed 98 pounds when he was liberated."

"We couldn't get a car right after the war even if we did have the money; they weren't available," Daphne said. "We put our name on the list at a dealership in San Antonio for a second-hand car. We were about 200 down on that list. We didn't get a car until 1947.

"But we lived with so much love. It's hard to describe how poor everybody was. This war followed ten years of Depression. Nobody had anything. At least we didn't know anybody who did. We didn't realize just how poor we were. When everybody's in the same shape it looks normal.

"Obviously if you became that poor after experiencing the kind of prosperity we have today, you'd be very aware of your poverty. But we weren't. We didn't expect a whole lot.

"By the way, I finally learned to ride a bicycle after my husband came back from the war. He taught me how in Brackenridge Park in San Antonio."

"Tell me some more things about the world that have changed since then," I said.

"Americans are so materialistic now," Dorothy said.

"That's right," Freda said. "Everybody has two cars, two TVs, and a computer. Back then a family was lucky to have one car and a radio."

"We have no memory, that's changed!" Rubye said, setting off another chorus of laughter.

Buddy Lewis
Lewisville

"**I**t looked like I wasn't going to be drafted, so I went down to see the recruiters," Buddy Lewis told me. "But I didn't want to go in as a buck private because I needed extra money to help my folks out. My parents were old and my daddy couldn't work, so a lot of my earnings went to take care of them. As a private I'd only make $50 a month, so I wanted to find a way to get into the service at a higher rate.

"The recruiting offices from all the branches stood right next to each other, so I went down the line. First I asked the Marines what they could do and they said, 'Oh yeah, we'll take you, we'll make you a corporal in two months.' I said, 'Well, that's an easy decision. I'll go see what somebody else will do.'

"See, I knew the recruiters could make me any promise they want, but once I got into boot camp, who knows what's really going to happen to me?

"The next office over was the Coast Guard. They said, 'We can give you a carpenter's mate rate right now.' I said, 'That's what I want.' That paid $26 a month more than I

Carpenter's Mate First Class Everette G. (Buddy)
Lewis works in the carpenter's shop of LST 887.

would have gotten the other way. I never even made it to
the next office, the Navy recruiter."

"Good for you," I said, impressed. I'd never heard of
somebody negotiating his pay before joining the military!

"The Coast Guard never sent me to basic training. They
put me to work repairing boats and building offices at
Curtis Bay, Maryland. After a year and nine months of that I
told my superiors I wanted to go to sea."

"Why did you want to go?" I asked.

"I felt like my daddy had almost become ashamed of me. Other men were talking about their sons being over in the Pacific doing the fighting. Even though I was in the service, I was still in the States, doing a safe job. My daddy didn't *want* me to go, but he felt like I ought to go save the country just as much as anybody else. So, I think he felt better after I left Curtis Bay, and I felt good about going, too."

"Where did they send you?"

"First they had me go fight the Battle of New York." He laughed. "I sat there and waited at Ellis Island for six weeks before they assigned me to a ship.

"Eventually they sent me to LST school at Camp Bradford, Virginia. We learned everything there was to know about an LST (Landing Ship - Tank). I learned how to shallow-dive and cut metal underwater. Then we went on a three-week shakedown cruise in the Chesapeake Bay.

"A carpenter's mate doesn't have much to do aboard an LST. There's no wood. Everything is made of metal. So I learned how to weld and cut with an acetylene torch.

"My girlfriend, Addiebell Herring, came to meet me in Pittsburgh when I went there to join my ship. I told her beforehand, 'No matter what I say or do, let's get married.'

"We'd been engaged for a while but had decided we wouldn't get married just yet. I couldn't see getting married and then going overseas. But after the cruise on the Chesapeake, I thought, 'Hell, if I'm going to the Pacific Ocean, I would like to leave something behind.' She met me up there and we got married.

"We picked up our LST, No. 887, at a shipyard on the Ohio River. All the women who had come to visit their

LST 887's crew poses for a group portrait. Lewis is the tallest man in the center of the back row. At 6'4", he was the tallest member of the crew.

LST 887 is launched at a shipyard in Pittsburgh.

LST 887 goes through its commissioning
ceremony on Nov. 7, 1944, in New Orleans.

husbands or boyfriends watched us take over the ship. We
took her down the Ohio, then down the Mississippi River to
New Orleans, then out into the Gulf for a shakedown
cruise. My wife met me there in New Orleans for three or
four more days and then we headed to the Pacific. We went
through the Panama Canal and on up to Seattle, Washington, where we picked up a load of tanks and armored
vehicles.

"We stopped in Hawaii. One night I went out with some
other fellas to explore the island; we were out on a street-
car drinking Tom Collinses, and that night I thought

131

mosquitoes were just eating my legs, and I couldn't figure out why. I'd get up, shoo them away, lay back down, and they just kept coming back.

"The next morning, I couldn't see out of my eyes, couldn't put my shoes on, and my hands were about two inches thick. I had the hives. I swelled up like a toad. A doctor gave me a shot and said, 'We'll let you go back to the States if you want to.'

"I said, 'No, I can't go back to the States. I'll stay on my ship.'

"We headed to the invasion of Okinawa. On the way, one of the Army boys we were carrying started acting strangely. So they placed him under guard."

"Strangely how?" I asked.

"Like he was mentally disturbed. Two guards were standing watch over him, and he knocked both of them unconscious and jumped overboard in the middle of the night."

"You mean, he committed suicide?"

"That's right. We looked for him but he was gone. All anybody heard was one holler, and then there was no sign of him. So the convoy went on its way."

"Why did he do it?"

"Could have been he was crazy and didn't understand what he was doing. Could have been he didn't want to go into combat. I don't know.

"Three days before we reached Okinawa, I went down with the mumps. I caught it from some soldiers in the next compartment. In fact I wrote a letter to my sister and she took the mumps from my letter!

"My station was on the bow. The first time we landed during the battle, I couldn't do my job because of the mumps. I stayed down below. I had a jock strap and swimming trunks on to protect myself down there. You know, your mumps go down there, and you can have serious problems. I was in my bunk but I could hear everything going on outside. The noise was terrific. We had battlewagons all around us and whenever they let go with a salvo, we heard, actually we *felt,* a tremendous boom.

"But we landed on Okinawa twice during that battle, and I was able to help out the second time. My job was to open the doors and let the bow ramp down when we landed. I was out in the open, just aft of the twin 40mm guns. So I had a good view of everything going on. When the battlewagons shot their main guns, our ship would shake.

"Both times we landed there we brought in a load of men and equipment, hit the beach, unloaded, and backed off just as fast as we could. Then we anchored offshore with ships all around us, going to general quarters sometimes three or four times a day. Sometimes general quarters would end, and before we even got back to our compartment they'd call general quarters again.

"The second time we carried a load of aviation fuel to a Marine base. We got there in the evening and the Marines wanted to wait until the morning to unload. But we were a sitting duck out there with a load of fuel, and kamikaze planes and shells were landing all around us. So our skipper gave all the ship's liquor to the Marines to bribe them to take the fuel right away so we could get out of there. We were so close to shore, Japanese mortar fire hit the side of our ship. It left dents in the hull.

He shook his head, thinking back. "You can't believe the number of ships that were there. Wherever you looked. And the flak in the air was unbelievable.

"We had 13 Purple Hearts on our ship. Shrapnel hit some of our men. In fact some of them still have the metal in their body."

"Did you see any kamikazes attack where you were?" I asked.

"Yes. Once I was up topside watching and I saw a kamikaze head straight for us. One of our men had been cleaning his 40mm on our stern, and he started shooting. The plane took some hits, veered to the left toward a Liberty ship, and struck it amidships on the port side. It exploded and went down into the drink. Fortunately, it didn't sink the Liberty ship."

"Could you see what was happening on land?"

"During the night I saw and heard ammunition dumps blow up, and oh, let me tell you, I *still* don't like fireworks because of that. Thank the Lord I didn't have to wade ashore like the Marines did. Of course our ship could have been sunk any time. Our saving grace was, we only drew 11 feet of water. We could go in close to shore, in the shallow water where no Japanese submarine could sneak up on us."

"Did you ever set foot on the island?"

"Only once, right after the end of the battle. I walked around with five or six guys and we explored a little village. We saw a young Japanese girl, a real cute little thing, trying to catch a chicken. She kept pointing to the chicken and saying to us, 'Shoot! Shoot!' They didn't have much to eat."

"Did you shoot it?"

"No. We didn't have a gun. We probably shouldn't have even been there. You know, our superiors didn't tell us we could wander into the villages, but they didn't tell us we couldn't either. Sometimes in the service, you're not sure you're allowed to be doing what you're doing, but if they didn't tell you not to do it, you figure it must be OK."

"What happened after Okinawa?"

"We spent the rest of the war moving all over the Pacific, hauling men and equipment from island to island. I saw a lot of remote islands during the war: Eniwetok, Ulithi, Manus, Russell Islands, Guadalcanal, Tulagi, Agrihan. We played a lot of basketball to pass the time. If we stopped at an island and another ship nearby had a basketball team, we'd play them.

"We went to Saipan three or four times during the war, and I'd watch the bombers coming in to land after missions over Japan. They'd fly right over our ship, and I'd look up and see holes in them that looked big enough to drop a bale of cotton through. How those planes stayed in the air I don't know."

"Where were you during the big typhoon of June 1945?" I asked.

"We were off Saipan when that happened. Afterwards we saw a flattop come in with the flight deck rolled back over to the bridge. The cruiser USS *Pittsburgh* came in with its entire bow missing. It passed by us on the way to Guam for repairs."

"How did it stay afloat with its bow missing?" I asked.

"It had waterproof compartments and shipfitters who went to work real fast to keep her afloat," he said.

"Tell me what life was like aboard ship," I requested.

"I can tell you I was an old man on that ship. Everybody was 17, 18, 19, and I was 30. We had one little boy, just 17 years old; he froze on his gun during our first air raid. He later turned into a good gunner.

"One thing was amusing at the time, but later I found out it wasn't so funny. A crewmember got drunk on Guadalcanal. One of our lieutenants had sold him a fifth of whiskey for $100. They court-martialed the boy, and one of the lieutenants on the board that court-martialed him was the one who sold him the damned whiskey. That's one of the dirtiest things I ever saw. I couldn't believe the guy would do it.

"Also on Guadalcanal, one of the boys stole a jeep and brought it on the ship. I didn't have anything to do with it. I don't know how they snuck it up there. When we went to another island the skipper took over the jeep and used it to ride around on. He wouldn't let the boys use it. The boys retaliated by taking the rotor out of the engine. And somebody composed a song and sang it over the loudspeakers, 'Who stole the rotor from the motor?'

"The Army caught up with us, and we had to unload the jeep and give it to them. It was a fun ship. We were like a bunch of kids, just doing whatever came natural. We weren't extreme military, and we didn't have to dress out in whites. Over on the Navy ship next to us they'd have everyone dressed in whites, and our men wore dungarees cut off at the hips.

"I was lucky, I had good duty. If I ever went back I'd want to go on the same type of ship. I liked it. I knew every foot of it."

Buddy Lewis today.

"Why is it that the Coast Guard was involved in combat operations so far from home?" I asked.

"They just call it the Coast Guard, they don't specify *which* coast," he said wryly. "The Coast Guard has participated in every war the United States has been involved in. We traveled side by side with the Navy... except one time; the lead ship headed the wrong way and my executive officer refused to follow. He went the way he was supposed to go, and the Navy caught up with us later. Coast Guardsmen are good sailors."

I was all right, just almost drowned is all

Sam Holder
Lubbock

"**W**hen the war started I was already in Iceland with the 6th Marines," Sam Holder told me. "I had enlisted in June 1940, and we shipped out in the spring of 1941 from San Diego through the Panama Canal, to Charleston, South Carolina, and then on to Reykjavik, Iceland. We pulled into the harbor there at 2 a.m., and the sun was just setting."

"Why did they send you there?" I asked.

"The U.S. thought the Germans might attack Iceland's east coast, and we were sent there as a precautionary measure. Only one highway crossed from the east coast to the west coast, and it went through a high mountain pass. They put thirty of us up there for a month. Our intelligence indicated the German army would come down that highway if it invaded Iceland. We had orders to stop them. And we had orders not to retreat."

"*Thirty* of you?"

"Thirty."

"Okay..."

"We set up machine guns on both sides of the pass overlooking the highway and waited. We were ready for them, but fortunately they never showed up."

Sam Holder in 1944.

"What did you think of Iceland?" I asked.

"Not a very good place. There's not a tree on Iceland, not even a bush. It's a volcanic rock. The winters are really cold, and the wind there sometimes blows over 100 miles an hour. We lived in Quonset huts with dirt piled up on each side so the wind wouldn't blow them away. We spent most of our time there digging trenches and unloading ships. It wasn't very much fun."

"Did you get much chance to interact with the Icelandic people?"

"I wouldn't say they were too friendly. I got the impression they didn't like us being there. I was single then, and they had some pretty good-looking girls, but they didn't want much to do with the Marines. We were about 12 miles outside of Reykjavik, and I only went to town one time."

"Why?"

"There wasn't anything to do. No nightlife.

"The Quonset huts had coal stoves for heating. Six men lived in one hut, and each night one man would have to stay awake and keep the fire going because it was so cold! Iceland wasn't much fun.

"Then the Japanese bombed Pearl Harbor, and soon after that we returned to San Diego. The Marine Air Corps was forming up and asking for volunteers, and I joined it. We shipped out from there to the Pacific.

"This was a nightmare. They crammed 4,600 of us onto a ship designed to accommodate perhaps 1,800. We slept in bunks down in the hold in little 8' by 10' rooms with twelve or fifteen bunks, stacked up six high. It was terrible.

"As we left San Diego I sat up on the top deck with a Marine who'd already been overseas. I asked him, 'Do you ever get seasick?' He said, 'No.'

"I said, 'Well, I feel kind of woozy.'

"He advised me, 'Don't think about it. You should go down to your bunk and lay flat on your back and close your eyes and tell yourself you won't get seasick.' I tried that and sure enough it worked. I never did get seasick during the whole war.

"We only got two meals a day, and we had to stand in line four hours to eat. Some of us went hungry much of the time; with so many people on board, it sometimes became impossible to make it to the mess. They served nothing but oatmeal for breakfast and mutton stew for supper. Every night, mutton stew. I ate so much mutton stew I still can't stand the thought of it.

"Sometimes we'd just skip a meal because we were sick of standing in line. Sometimes somebody would get their hands on some candy bars—we called them nickel candy bars back then—and those things would sell for $5.

"We stopped briefly in Samoa, just dropped anchor off shore, and some natives paddled canoes out to the ship and offered us coconuts. We put money in a metal bucket and lowered it down on a rope, and they sent the coconuts up. We had twenty coconuts for 4,600 men.

"I managed to get a fourth of a coconut. Way up on the top deck of the ship, we had life rafts stacked against the rail. It created a sort of cave you could crawl under to hide, and I decided to hide under there so I'd get a chance to eat all my coconut.

"I crawled back under there and started to take a bite and I heard this voice say, 'Give me a bite, Sam!' Somebody saw me and followed me in there! Anyway, I managed to get a bite. We really did go hungry on that ship.

"Sleeping down in those little rooms was so uncomfortable, I always took my blanket and pillow up on the top deck. A lot of people did that."

"How comfortable was it up on the deck?" I asked.

"It wasn't very nice," he said. "The deck was very hard. But it was better than sleeping with a bunch of snoring men in a tiny room! We could crawl under a lifeboat in case it rained. Sometimes we'd throw a lifeboat down on the deck and sleep in it.

"Finally we reached New Caledonia, a French island. We camped 20 miles outside of Noumea, the capital. We took our machetes and started to clear away the jungle on the bank of a river. Took us several weeks to get it cleaned out. The mosquitoes were so bad, you could take your hand and rake down your arms and get a handful of mosquitoes. But the good thing was, they weren't the malaria-bearing kind of mosquitoes. They were harmless, unless you count all the biting.

"We cut down trees and I built a mess hall and dining hall for enlisted men and officers. I built the officers' quarters. All the buildings were built with logs and thatched roofs. The enlisted men lived in large tents with wooden floors.

"Finally we had a place to live with a beautiful view of the river. We built a raft and put it down on the river for the men to bathe and swim. This river was about 12 feet deep, and it was so clear we could drop a quarter in and see it on the bottom.

"At this time I was a sergeant. An old French lady lived across the river; we got to calling her Mama. She owned some land and raised cattle and sheep. She got to know me real well, called me Sam-*ee*. She sold liquor and wine to the troops, but when the officers got wind of that they declared her place off limits. I was the sergeant of the guard and had to post a sentry over there at night to make sure none of the boys went over there. Part of my job was to go check on the guards during the night to make sure they were OK, so whenever I went over there she gave me a bottle of wine or whiskey. She wouldn't take any money for it. She was real good to me.

"This lady's son had a boat for sale, a sailboat with an auxiliary motor, so I bought it along with two other men. Sometimes on a Saturday we'd load the boat up with groceries and take it two miles downriver to the ocean and explore dozens of little islands out there. We'd fish for sea bass and sea trout and sleep out there on one of the islands."

"I'll bet you got a really good view of the stars out there," I said.

"Yes, and they looked really close. It was beautiful. New Caledonia was real nice. It never freezes there; the temperature always stays between the mid-60s and mid-70s year round.

"I slept on the sand close to the water one night, and when I woke up the next morning I saw a five-foot coral snake laying right next to me, only three feet away. Coral snakes are real deadly. You never saw somebody jump up and run away so fast!"

"What was your unit doing there on New Caledonia?" I asked.

"VMJ-253 was a squadron of C-47 Dakota cargo planes. We flew supplies into Guadalcanal and a lot of other islands where we were fighting the Japs. We also had two fighter planes for protection.

"We had good times on New Caledonia. But we didn't go into Noumea much, not much to do there. We didn't leave camp a whole lot. We were always busy, keeping the planes running.

"One day we were drinking beer with a lieutenant in the NCO club and he said, 'If you all could get a jeep, we could go see the nurses.' There was a camp full of nurses three miles down the road. One of the guys worked in the motor pool, so he went and got us a jeep.

"We drove to the other camp and visited the nurses a while. Nothing much happened. We only stayed a little while and then decided to go back. When we pulled up to the gate of our camp, the armed guard there stopped us and said, 'You're all under arrest.'

"We said, 'What!? What for?' and he said, 'For taking a jeep without permission.'

"And we all turned and glared at the guy from the motor pool. He'd told us he had permission from his commanding officer to take it. He lied. So because of him, the lieutenant was confined to quarters for thirty days, and the rest of got busted a rank. I got busted from tech sergeant to staff sergeant. We were innocent; we didn't know. The commanding officer told me, 'If you keep your nose clean, I'll see that you get this rank back in thirty days.' And he did."

"You must have been pretty mad at that guy."

"Oh, yeah. We never would have gone if we'd known the truth. Anyway, when I wrote my mom I would usually put 'Tech Sgt. Samuel A. Holder' on the letter. I didn't want her to know I'd been busted, so rather than saying 'Staff Sgt. Samuel A. Holder' I just wrote 'Sgt. Samuel A. Holder,' you know, being vague. But I didn't fool her. She wrote back, 'What'd you get busted for?'

"One day, we don't know where he came from, but a Jap appeared out of nowhere and dashed through the camp, in broad daylight. Lots of us took shots at him, but nobody got him. He jumped into the river and swam away. We never figured out where he came from; Japanese forces weren't that close by. He might have been a deserter, or he might have been spying on us.

"I advanced pretty fast. I was a corporal when I arrived on New Caledonia. In two years I had six stripes.

"The island had lots of small farms, and we had lots of beer. I'd load a few cases of beer onto my jeep, drive up the island, and trade beer for fresh fruit and vegetables. Sometimes I got live chickens and we'd have fried chicken that night. We ate so good in the enlisted mess, some of the officers started coming down to eat with us!" He laughed. "I guess they didn't have anybody going out and finding fresh food for them.

"The New Caledonians, both the Kanak natives and the French, got along really well with us Americans. The Kanak farmers were always glad to get some beer; they didn't have any way out there in the woods. I'd take my jeep and drive deep into the woods on winding, unpaved roads through heavy vegetation to find them.

"We used to go deer hunting with a chief of the natives, an old black man. He'd guide us through the woods, clearing a path through the brush for us. Once I was following him through the woods and saw a huge spider, the size of your fist, hanging in our path. This old chief just picked it up with his bare hand and tossed it to the side! He explained, 'There are no poisonous spiders on New Caledonia.'

"Down the river we had a bridge. One day one of the fighter pilots flew his plane under it! He couldn't have had more than two inches clearance on each side. That was the craziest thing I ever saw anybody do. Don't know why he did it, maybe just to say he could. Maybe he was bored. There wasn't much in the way of entertainment there. We didn't have a lot to do but shoot the sharks."

"Excuse me?"

"Yeah, we'd shoot the sharks. I went down to the beach with my .45 and a bunch of ammunition in my big heavy dungarees. The sharks swam in close to the shore, and we'd shoot at them.

"One day while I was down at the beach there came a real heavy rain. I don't know why I did it, but I walked back on the wrong side of the river. I ended up across from the camp, and I decided to swim across. I jumped in wearing my dungarees and boots, with a pistol and lots of ammo in my pockets.

"But the heavy rain had swollen the river and it was running real swift. Weighted down like I was, swimming across was harder work than I expected. I got halfway across and realized I couldn't make it.

"I thought 'Well, if I go down to the bottom and get this heavy pistol and ammunition off, maybe I can make it.' I went down there and tried to undress but I got excited, panicked, couldn't get nothing off. I came back up, floating fast toward the ocean and just about exhausted.

"Then I looked up and noticed two of my buddies, Jack Daws and Tim Spencer, on the dock getting ready to go swimming. I yelled at them as loud as I could, 'Help me! Help me!' And they heard me. They'd already taken their clothes off, so they jumped in the water naked and with the river flowing so fast, they got to me real quick. I passed out just before they reached me.

"They pulled me onto the bank and pumped the water out of my lungs and I came to. I was all right, just almost drowned is all.

"It was stupid, thinking I could swim across a rain-swollen river with the dungarees, boots, pistol, and ammo," he said ruefully. "Just the dungarees alone would have been enough to weigh me down once they got soaked. If those two boys hadn't come down when they did, I wouldn't be here."

"What's your worst memory of the war?" I asked.

"The worst day of the whole war for me was the day one of our cargo planes took off for Sydney, Australia, and crashed just after takeoff near the edge of the water."

His voice dropped to a near whisper; I could tell he was going places he didn't want to go.

"A dozen men were killed, including a very close friend of mine, Leon Barr, who was from my hometown of

Sam Holder today.

Bakersfield, Calif. Thirty of us had to go out in small boats to search for the bodies. The plane sat in shallow water, half submerged. We searched around there for quite a while but I don't believe we found all the men. I hauled bodies aboard our boat. It was really rough. They never figured out what caused the crash.

"After the war I went to visit his parents. I told them I was a really good friend of Leon's, and we talked about him for a while. He was their only child."

Whenever they shoot one round
at you, send fifty back at them

Jim Hansen
Longview

"**B**efore the war started I tried my hand at a variety of jobs," Jim Hansen told me. "I got hired to be a machinist, but the first thing they told me was, 'Don't touch any equipment you don't know how to use.' Naturally I didn't know how to do anything, so they wouldn't let me touch anything. They just had me sweep the floors. After a couple of days of that I decided, 'I don't think I'm cut out to be a machinist.'

"I hitchhiked with Butch Johnson, a buddy of mine, down to a recreation area at Arnolds Park, Iowa, on the shores of Lake Okoboii. We looked around for work. The carnival had plenty of jobs, but they didn't pay anything. Finally we walked down through a residential neighborhood where people had their summer cabins, and a man hired us to mow his lawn. He offered us $10 apiece to mow it once a week. Now that was a lot of money back in 1941. So we took that job, mowed his lawn right away, and that gave us each $10 to walk around with.

"We walked around some more and came up to a roller skating rink. It had a big Help Wanted sign out front, so we

Jim Hansen in February 1945, when he was promoted to 2nd lieutenant.

went in and applied. The manager asked if we could skate. Well, he didn't specify whether he meant ice skate or roller skate. So we said we could. We could *ice* skate, you see. We'd never been on roller skates in our life."

"Uh-oh . . ." I said.

"The first night we worked there we had to put skates on the customers. When they came in they got a ticket and they gave it to whoever put their skates on. At the end of the night, the manager paid us two cents a ticket. And that added up to quite a bit of money. He had a big crowd every night.

"He told us, 'After you get everybody's skates on, put yours on and get out there on the floor and help people.' When it looked like nobody else was coming in we put our skates on, and I kind of rolled up to the edge of the floor and didn't know how in the world I was gonna get up to the speed everybody else was going. I gave a big run and jumped out on the floor and down I went. I tripped everybody up."

"Did he fire you?"

"No, but he made us stay after work every night and gave us lessons until three o'clock in the morning. We had a fun summer there. Big bands played every night at two big dance halls, and we'd go dance after work. We spent the summer there and finally one day I said, 'You know, Butch, we're experts at roller skating, riding roller coasters, and going to dances. I think it's time for me to look for something else to do.'

"I hitchhiked home and got my little suitcase, and my dad asked, 'Where you going?' I said, 'Well, I don't know where I'm going right now, but there's more to this old world than them 230 acres out there.' We lived on a farm, see.

"I hitchhiked to California and got a job working for Douglas Aircraft in Long Beach."

"What did you do?"

"I installed firewalls. My job was to put a metal shield on the nacelle between the motor and the wing, to keep the wing from catching fire if a fire broke out in the motor."

"Where did you get qualified for a job like that?" I asked.

"I lied an awful lot back then." He laughed. "I figured if anybody else can learn a job I can too, so I just told them I knew how to do it."

"Wow," I said admiringly, thinking maybe I should try that sometime. "How did it go on the first day?"

"The first day it quickly came to light that I didn't know anything about anything. But I was willing to learn. In six months I made group leader of that department. They also put another job on me; I was to mount the engines and torque them. I had ten men working for me. So, that's where I spent the first part of the war. I stayed there a year and a half, and then I got drafted in June 1942.

"They took me to Fort Crook, Nebraska, for my physical. That was quite an eye-opener for a farm boy. The Army buildings were huge, nothing but long hallways and rooms. Everything was numbered. I guess that's where the saying 'by the numbers' came from. The hallways were numbered, the rooms were numbered, equipment was numbered, even people were numbered.

"I passed the physical all right. Had a big time doing that; got in quite a bit of trouble because I couldn't keep from laughing at everything. We had to get a hemorrhoid test. If you had any modesty, the Army took that away from you. They lined a bunch of us up against the wall, and a corporal said, 'No. 7, bend over and spread your cheeks.'

"And he said, 'I've got 'em spread.' I looked down the line, and he had a hold of his cheeks on his face. Then I got in trouble for laughing.

"I got in trouble all the time, you know. They didn't allow any laughing. The corporal said, 'No. 3, this is serious business. Don't you know there's a war going on?' I said, 'Well, I heard a rumor.' And then I was in trouble again.

"We walked around in the buff for the entire physical. And it was pretty dad-burned cold in there. So on the way home on the bus I got deathly sick. I got back to Rock Rapids, Iowa, where the draft board was, and they told me to call my parents. I said, 'I don't believe I can holler that loud, they're 30 miles away.'

"He said to call them on the telephone. I said, 'We don't have a telephone. We wanted one but couldn't get one because there's no telephone line running past our farm.'

"So they put me up in a hotel and called a doctor and he gave me a shot, and I felt great the next morning. They took me home and I stayed there about two weeks until I got orders to report to the draft board again. The same crowd congregated there that had congregated when we left for our physicals. They loaded us onto a bus for the train station, families and all. So many people were trying to get into the train station, half of them were stuck sitting outside in the parking lot."

"How did your family take your leaving?" I asked.

"They took it pretty good, kept a smile on their faces for my sake. My mother, father, four brothers, and one sister had all come. But with everyone else, it was a lot of crying and carrying on, and I couldn't figure out what everybody was so unhappy about. I always liked to do new things, so I was excited.

"See, when I left the farm, I lost my farm deferment. My brothers still had theirs. I was the only brother who left, the only one who wanted to go out into the world. I had no regrets whatsoever about leaving. I worked real hard on the farm, in fact I had a terrible time getting through high school, because the work had to be done before anybody went to school. So I missed a lot of classes.

"I had a coach who'd bring my lessons out to the farm on Monday mornings, all my tests and everything. He told my mother what tests I was to take and when, and then he'd come out on Friday evening and take them back.

"I never did get to practice any of the sports. Everything just came kind of natural to me. I played first base on the baseball team, center on the basketball team, and never got to practice any of it. I missed a lot of the baseball games because they played in the afternoon. I got to play every basketball game, though. The coach would draw pictures of the formations he wanted us to use and I would memorize them."

"So even though you were going to war, you were pretty glad to leave the farm," I said.

"Yes. I wasn't a farmer, never could claim that I was. I got my train car assignment and thought I was lucky because I got a sleeper car, but they crammed so many people in there we couldn't make up the bunks. We had to take turns sitting and standing. The train took us to Fort Leavenworth, Kansas, where they loaded us up on the open backs of trucks and drove us around camp in a cold, misty rain. I'll never forgive that officer for doing that to us because we had no rain gear, no protection at all.

"We finally got to our barracks. They called our names out and told us which NCO we were supposed to report to. Ours was an adhesive-tape corporal."

"What's that?" I asked.

"He was a private under limited service and wouldn't ever leave the camp, so they couldn't make him a corporal. So they just pretended he was a corporal and put his stripes on with adhesive tape. And he kept those stripes pulled forward where we could all see them.

"My buddies and I got bunks upstairs. We had to make up our bunks and pull the blankets tight, and the corporal would take the half-dollar and bounce it off the blanket. If it didn't bounce up high enough where he could catch it, he tore the bed up and we had to remake it.

"This little corporal gave us a demonstration on how to make up the bunks, and we all went back to our bunks and made them up like he showed us. But when he started bouncing the half-dollar, nobody passed the test. He tore up all of our bunks.

"So I said, 'Sergeant, if you'll show me one more time I believe I can do it.' Well, I had this corporal going my way when I called him Sergeant. So he showed us one more time, but before he could tear it up I grabbed my own half-dollar and bounced it off the blanket, and it only bounced up three or four inches; everybody just about died laughing.

"Well...he got mad. He said to all of us, 'You're gonna get punishment for that.' I said, 'Don't punish them, punish me, I was the one that did it.' He said, 'No, they laughed. You're all going to get it.'

"The next morning at four he woke us up by blowing a whistle and told us to stack everything on our bunks because we were gonna scrub the floor. And since I caused the whole thing I had to go down to the latrine and bring up three buckets of water and brushes and soap. We started scrubbing, and he stood at the head of the stairs loudly discussing our ancestry.

"He said, 'I have to report to the first sergeant. This better be clean when I get back.' He headed down the stairs. I knew the path to the orderly room led right underneath the window on the left side of the barracks. So I had my buddy open the window and I peeked out. I had my bucket of water with me. He walked right underneath me and I dumped the whole bucket on him. I hit him dead center."

"No way," I said.

"I quickly ran around to everybody's buckets and got a little water from each one of them. We heard him hit the bottom of those stairs and stumble and fall and crawl all the way up. He checked everybody's bucket to see who was out of water, but we all had the same amount.

"So he restricted us. We couldn't leave the barracks. They blew the whistle about seven that morning for everybody to fall out. Of course my group didn't leave the barracks because we'd been restricted. Here comes the first sergeant wanting to know what in the world was going on. He blew the whistle, didn't we hear it? One guy told him,

'Yes, Sergeant, we heard it. But we're restricted to the barracks.' So the sergeant countermanded that order.

"My group ended up in Camp Maxey, right outside of Paris, Texas. All that greeted us when the train stopped was a little four-by-four depot. We sat there in the train for 45 minutes. Nobody entered the car, nobody said nothing. We just sat there and looked at each other. Finally an officer got onto the train and told us to disembark and he would give us our orders outside. We started to get up and then he started hollering, *'Everybody double time!'* We just looked at each other. We didn't know what double time meant.

"Finally he got us all running. We ran down to a motor pool and got on four big trucks. Of course it was a cold misty rain again. We rode around for a while and when we got off we were told, 'When your name is called I will give you your company, battalion, and regiment. There'll be a sergeant waiting who will step forward and raise his hand.'

"Each one of us was loaded down with two big duffel bags. When my name was called, my sergeant stepped out, way down the line. I grabbed my two bags and tried to run, but it was nothing that even looked like running. All the sergeants started screaming at me. Every sergeant I passed would scream in my face. When I got to my sergeant I collapsed on top of my two bags, and he hollered, 'Get up and get those bags up double time!'

"I said, 'Sergeant, if you want those damn bags double time, be my guest!'"

"You didn't," I said.

"I did. He glared down at me and finally he just broke into a grin and said, 'Aw, I'll carry one. It's better than carrying you and both bags.' He helped me and we walked to the company barracks. Once we got there he put his hands on his hips and got nose to nose with me, and said, 'If you ever talk to me like that again I'll eat you alive.'

"I said, 'Yes sir.' He screamed, 'You don't say sir to a non-commissioned officer; you call them by their rank. Don't say sir!' So I said, 'Yes sir!'

"I was the only man in the company for two weeks, so the sergeant had me all to himself. He took me to the supply room and got all my bedding and equipment issued to me. I went upstairs and made up my bunk. He asked, 'You know how to make your bunk up?' I said, 'Oh, after a fashion.'

"I'd found out the secret to that half-dollar trick was to have a real thick, stiff mattress. And I had one. I pulled that bedding as tight as a fiddle string. He said, 'OK, I'll check it.' But before he had a chance I whipped out my own half dollar and flopped it on that bed real quick and it bounced three feet in the air, and he caught it, grinned, and said, 'Well I guess I don't have to check that.'

"Every night I had to do close order drill, just me and the sergeant. He marched me up and down the barracks until 11 o'clock at night. He was practicing giving orders on me. This was a brand new division just starting up, the 102nd Infantry. Very few recruits had arrived at this point. Let me tell you, that barracks was a mighty lonesome place to sleep all by yourself.

"They issued me the pride of the Army, the M-1 Garand rifle. Oh, I was proud of that thing. I'd done an awful lot of hunting when I was a little kid. It was my job to put meat on the table during the Depression years. But that was with a .22, nothing like this.

"I was so proud of that gun, but I didn't know anything about it when they handed it to me. Two days later I knew that thing backward and forward. I had to strip it down, wash it, put it together. They'd make me leave the area and they'd tear that thing into as many pieces as they could, and I'd have to come back and put it back together.

"Then the other recruits started coming in, and before long we had a full company, about two hundred men. I was in 1st Platoon, Fox Company, 2nd Battalion, 405th Regiment, 102nd Infantry Division. The training started, and that got to be rough. They'd fall us in about four o'clock in the morning and make us take a 25-mile hike. That was tough. A lot of the men just collapsed to the ground. They weeded out the ones who were not physically fit to be in the infantry. The training completely broke down a lot of men in their mid-thirties. I was twenty years old, and I thought they were gonna break me. But I stayed with them.

"We did maneuvers in Louisiana. My platoon sergeant went AWOL right before they started, and as a private first class I was the ranking member in the platoon. Nobody else in the platoon had any rank yet. So at the age of twenty with four months of service under my belt, I became platoon sergeant. I found out I'd been promoted when the captain asked me, 'Can you handle taking these men on maneuvers, Sergeant?' I said, 'I'll give it a whirl, Captain, and if I can't you'll be the first to know.' But I made out all right.

"We went on maneuvers with the 99th, 75th, and 84th divisions. I got three boats for my platoon to cross the Red River. We plopped 'em all in the water and jumped into them, and when we all got in, the boats were sitting on the bottom of the river. So I took a stand up at the front of the boat like George Washington did when he was crossing the Delaware, and the men all got to singing, 'Row row row your boat.'

"That went over like a lead balloon with the captain. He started hollering at us to get across that river, so we all just stepped out of the boats into the river and walked across.

"We were attacking the enemy, and one of my squad leaders hollered at me, 'Sergeant, I'm minus one man.' I told him to send two men back to find the missing one. The two men finally caught up with him and brought him back, and that old boy was mud from one end to the other. What happened was, he thought he'd wash his boots off after he crossed the river, and he came up to this little sinkhole, started washing them off, and realized he'd stepped into quicksand. And he couldn't get out. When they found him he was up to his butt. He got punished that night; he had to dig a six-by-six-by-six for leaving the platoon during combat."

"What was a six-by-six-by-six?" I asked.

"When somebody broke a rule, they made him dig a hole six feet long, six feet wide, and six feet deep. After he dug the hole the sergeant would either spit or piss in it, and then he'd have to fill it back up."

"That's a pretty harsh punishment," I observed.

"This was not the modern day Army," Hansen said. "This was the survival of the fittest Army. I give thanks every day that I was mentally and physically prepared when I went in.

"Eventually we boarded a train for Fort Dix, New Jersey. On the way we passed through New Orleans, and our train got too close to the troop train ahead of us so we took a three-hour layover. The battalion commander came up with the bright idea to let everybody go into town for one and a half hours. Well, that's the wrong thing to do in New Orleans!

"All the troops went uptown. Four hours later, nobody had reported back to the train. I found most of my platoon and took them back to the train, and the commander sent us back out to find the ones who hadn't shown up. Well, when we got back uptown we forgot what we was up there for, and we started having a good time again!" He laughed.

"Finally the MPs circled all of us and got us back in the train except for two men. They didn't let us off the train again for the rest of the trip. When we reached Fort Dix, the two men we'd left behind were waiting for us. They'd hitchhiked and beat us there.

"Before we could move into our barracks we found out the camp was eaten up with body lice. Everybody caught it. They brought blue ointment in by the truckload and shaved everybody, got the barracks disinfected, and we moved in.

"We had our showdown inspection to make sure we had everything we needed. One man in my platoon had a habit of going AWOL every time I assigned him to scrub the barracks.

"A lot of men would call back to get an extension when they were out on furlough. Well, this man Fisher was the type who would call back for an extension when he was AWOL. He called me one night and said, 'Well Sarge, what's the situation?' I said, 'Fisher, you better come on back now, in the morning they're checking our equipment and you've got to have everything.' Next morning I walked into the squad room and there he was in his bunk sound asleep. He went overseas with us. We caught a ferry out to our passenger ship, the SS *General Anderson*. Each one of us had about 40 pounds of gear more than we were physically capable of carrying. When we went under the bow of the ship I looked up and saw the name and said, 'At least it's a passenger ship.' I figured it wouldn't be too uncomfortable. But we had to go four decks below the waterline to find our place and it was HOT. Only about 14 inches separated the bunks and we had to crawl into them horizontally. Since the ship wasn't moving, the air wasn't circulating. As soon as I got everything on my bunk and made sure my whole platoon was there, I hurried up on deck to get some air.

"Later, back down below, all of a sudden I felt air coming through the vent and I felt the ship moving. By that time it was pretty late, so I went to sleep. I had the top bunk and that cool air was hitting me real good, and I went into a deep sleep until morning.

"I got up and went up on deck and looked around and all I could see was ships. I'd guess about two hundred. We tried to count them but they continued clear over the horizon. No land in sight. Troop carriers stayed in the center of the convoy so enemy subs couldn't get to us. Cargo ships surrounded us. Battlewagons followed along way off in the distance, but destroyers constantly steamed in and out all through the convoy. Every time a ship detected what they thought was a submarine, here come those destroyers. Those ships could really move. Seemed like every time I woke up we were having a submarine alert, but our convoy didn't lose any ships.

"After a brief stop during the night at Weymouth, England, we landed in Cherbourg, France. We were the first troops to unload directly from a troop carrier in the big port there after the Normandy invasion.

"We got on trucks, but we didn't ride more than four or five miles when they ordered us to stop and unload. Patton needed the trucks and the gas. So we cussed him some, because now we had to walk and carry that big load.

"We finally got to where we were going at three or four o'clock in the morning, and when they yelled Halt, everybody fell right where they were standing. We lay there out in the countryside and didn't even bother to set up tents the first night we were there. I still had my pack on when I woke up the next morning. I think we had walked 20 miles, carrying all the gear."

"What were you carrying?" I asked.

"Equipment for the company headquarters. Another boy and I had the field desk for the headquarters between us. It's a very heavy two-by-two desk with drawers, a square box with handles on each side. That was where they kept the combat records. I also had my M-1 slung over the other shoulder.

"Orders came down that we would furnish drivers for the quartermasters. Those guys were the ones who were supposed to deliver all the supplies to the front line. But for some reason the supplies didn't seem to be reaching the combat troops. Our troops were running out of ammunition, gasoline, boots. Everything was leaving the coastal areas, but it wasn't reaching the troops.

"So the Army conducted a big investigation and found out the drivers of these quartermaster trucks would stop in the big towns and sell everything off the back of the truck. Sometimes they even sold the truck. The solution: They recruited a bunch of our men to ride shotgun on these trucks."

"Did it help?" I asked.

"It worked out well. They found out what we were doing and why we were there, and a lot of the original drivers never did get to the end of the line or, for some reason or another, never got back to their units. After a while just about the only truck drivers they had were soldiers from the 102nd Infantry. And we got the supplies where they needed to be. Finally the quartermaster drivers decided they better straighten up, because there were a lot of them who never came back. I won't say what happened to them, but they never did get home again."

"Interesting," I said.

"After that we rode a train through Belgium into Holland and stopped in Heerlen. The train cars were called forty and eights, because they carried forty men or eight horses. They had no restroom facilities. The train traveled so slowly, when Mother Nature called we'd climb up on top of the boxcar, walk all the way up to the engine, jump off, tend to our needs, and get back on the train when our own car caught up with us.

"Also, nudity is not offensive there like it is here in America. So to get a shower, when it rained we just crawled up on top of the boxcar with a bar of soap and a towel, stripped off, and showered in the rain. And we often went through the middle of town like that."

"You're kidding," I said.

"The engineer got to where he'd play little tricks on us. Just before we got to a tunnel, he'd have the fireman throw in a bunch of coal and all that black smoke would roll out. He'd go through the tunnel real slow and fill it up with black smoke, and when ten or twenty cars were inside the tunnel, he'd just stop and let us breathe that black smoke for a while."

"Why in the world did he do that?" I asked.

"Just meanness. Of course, we was playing tricks on them so they got back at us."

"What kind of tricks?" I asked.

He paused. "We might have tried to unhook a car or something."

"No way!"

"Actually, we didn't just try. We *did* unhook the train right in the middle one time. He had to back up and hook up again!" He laughed.

"Finally, we got to Heerlen. From there the command we started hearing all the time was 'Spread out! Spread out!' If you got too close to your buddy you got hollered at. They didn't want one lucky mortar shell to hit and wipe out the whole company. They told us to stay about 10 yards from each other.

"We would move up on the line that night. The company commander briefed us that evening to reassure us. Right in the middle of his speech we heard an airplane come over, and all of a sudden we heard the whine of a bomb. Everybody dove for cover. I had been sitting on a little mound in front of a little ditch, about six inches deep. I rolled over into that, and four or five men jumped right on top of me. They all knew that little depression was there, but by the time they all stacked up on top of me they were sticking up about three feet in the air!

"The bomb hit about a mile and a half away. That's how good we were at judging the distance of incoming shells. Up on the line, we would eventually learn to tell where a shell would hit.

"After the bomb went off a bunch of guys came crawling out of the latrine and the sump pit. They cleaned up and we moved up that night to relieve a company from the 2nd Armored Division.

"A lieutenant from 2nd Armored met us and took us back to his squad leaders. Everything was hush-hush; nobody spoke. My platoon was placed on the very front line. Up until then we didn't even have an officer, but now a Lt. Greene arrived to take command of us. He told my platoon guide, the man directly under the platoon sergeant, to dig a foxhole for him while he went to visit company headquarters. My platoon guide was a big ol' Polish man from New Jersey. He said, 'Lieutenant, we're in combat now. You dig your own damn hole.'

"I said to myself, 'Uh-oh, Tom, you ain't long for this world.'

"The lieutenant came back from headquarters and sure enough nobody had dug his hole. He said to me, 'Sergeant, why didn't you have my hole dug?' I said, 'Lieutenant, you didn't tell me to have your hole dug, you told the platoon guide to do it. And I don't countermand orders from above.'

"Greene went to the platoon guide, who was sitting on his helmet and looked up and said, 'Sir, I told you once before, this is combat now. You dig your own damn hole.'"

"So did you guys dig him a hole?"

"Oh, we finally got him a hole dug. He helped. Figured it was the least he could do.

"The Army always stressed security. 'Don't say anything that could be overheard by somebody and used against us.' Well, we'd been on the line maybe an hour, and the Germans across the way cranked up their PA system and blared out in perfect English, 'We would like at this time to welcome the 102nd Infantry Division to the front line. We hope your stay will be a pleasant one.'

"And then they hit us with an artillery barrage like you wouldn't believe. I've never been so scared in my life. Afterwards I ran to all the foxholes to see if everybody had made it. I found a squad leader and asked, 'Is everybody in your squad all right?'

"He said, 'Yeah, I had two that went to diggin' deeper when the shells came in, and they dug so far down they were stuck down there. I had to shovel dirt back in so they could get out!'

"Fortunately, the artillery didn't hurt anybody.

"Then one night the Germans counterattacked. Artillery came first, right on top of us. The lieutenant said, 'Sergeant, I can't find anybody else; we're isolated from the company, and they need to know we're under attack.'

"I said, 'Lieutenant, the telephone line is down. But the noise is horrific. If they don't know by now we're under attack, they never will know.'

"He said, 'Well, I want you to run back and tell them. I'll be here. If you don't mind.'

"I said 'Aww, what the hell' and away I went. I ran to the platoon headquarters and found the telephone line that they had strung out from the company headquarters. I followed the wire. Shells landed so fast and furious and so close that when I heard one coming I'd fall on my belly and try to bury my head somewhere. And sometimes they hit so close, the blast rolled me over. The concussion was terrific. I'd have to lie there for a while and get my senses working again.

"I saw somebody coming towards me from the direction of company headquarters. I thought, 'He's gotta be one of us.' So I hollered at him and he stopped and said, 'Sgt. Hansen?' It was Corporal Souder, a communications man. He was out doing the same thing as me—trying to fix our telephone line. And the break was right there between us. He was holding the end of his line and I was holding the end of mine! So he patched them up and put his telephone on it, and I called the company commander.

"He says, 'How many men are there?' meaning Germans. I said 'Hell, I don't know, Captain, they're all over the damn place.'

"He said, 'Can we do anything to help?' I told him, 'No. We have them pinned down behind us; we're gonna try to hold them there until the German artillery starts shooting again.'

"The Germans used a rolling barrage when they had an attack going on. They'd keep the artillery out in front of their infantry as they attacked, and the infantry were supposed to return within a certain timeframe to their own line, and then the artillery would come back on top of us again. But we pinned down their infantry behind us so they couldn't get out, and their own artillery wiped them out. We counted about thirty dead, wounded, or just flat gave up.

"And that was our initiation into battle. That was really something, our first gun battle with the Germans and we came out way ahead of them. We didn't lose a man. After we whipped 'em that night they didn't bother us much.

"We could see a foxhole about two hundred yards out from us, and we couldn't figure out whether one or two Germans were in there. One night another boy and I crept out about a hundred yards, got down on our tummies, crawled past the hole, and came up to it from the rear. I peered over the edge of it and saw only one helmet. I motioned for my buddy to come up and help, and we reached down, grabbed him by the shoulders of his overcoat and yanked him out. We slammed him to the ground and I put my hand over his mouth so he couldn't holler. After he calmed down a little bit we grabbed him by the arms, lifted him up, and took off for our lines as hard as we could run.

"I thought I heard somebody crying. I said, 'Tom, what the hell was that sound?' He didn't know. So we stopped and squatted down and I took our prisoner's helmet off. I was never so shocked in my life. I asked him if he spoke English. He said yes. And I asked, 'How old are you?'

"He said, 'Fourteen.'"

"You've got to be kidding me," I said.

"No, I'm not kidding. I said, 'Good Lord.' We rested there for a minute and then managed to get back through our own lines without getting shot, and we took him back to company headquarters. The captain couldn't believe we went all the way out there and got him and he turned out to be a kid. The Germans sacrificed a fourteen-year-old just so he could warn them if an attack came through there. His

Sgts. Robert Lira and Bob Galloway from 2nd Platoon, Fox Company man a .50-caliber machine gun in the fall of 1944.

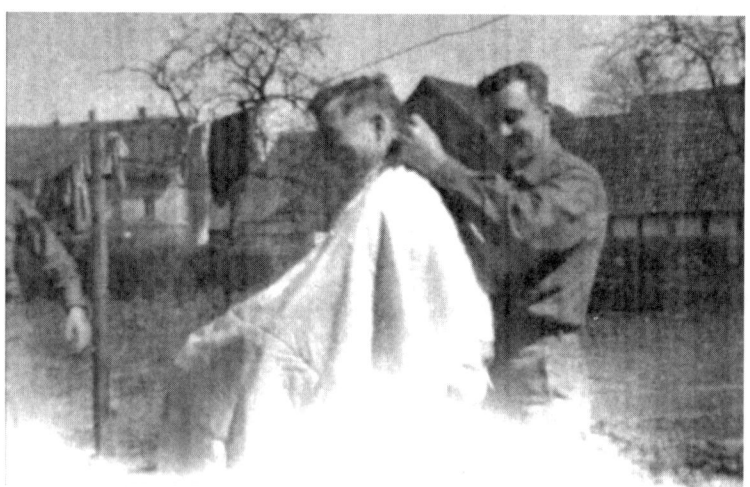

"The war was called to a temporary halt while I got a haircut," Jim Hansen jokes about this photo.

entire mission was, if we made a counterattack at night, he would call back to tell them we were on the way."

"What happened to him after that?" I asked.

"I don't know. We fought along the west bank of the Ruhr River for a long time, finally cleared the area. Then it came time to cross the river and invade the Ruhr Valley, the industrial area. We got our platoons built back up to full strength, and they brought in artillery and tanks. I saw tanks backed up hub to hub about a mile from the river in camouflage. We walked down to the edge of the river where the boats were supposed to be, but when we got there we couldn't find any boats.

"A Lt. Herrick was commanding our platoon now. Herrick said, 'Jim, take over the platoon, and I'll go see if I can find some boats.' We waited there but the artillery started coming in real thick. We took some casualties and there was nothing I could do about it sitting out there in the open. Couldn't go anywhere without boats. I decided we'd better get away from that river. I told the men to go back over the hill and take shelter in town.

"We got up the hill and were met by an eight-ball officer who'd been relieved of command and was just following along with battalion headquarters."

"What does eight-ball mean?"

"It means he was no longer qualified to lead troops into combat. He jumped up and called us cowards for leaving the scene of the battle. I said, 'Lieutenant, we took casualties down there that we didn't have to take. We couldn't find any boats down there. There's no use just sitting there and losing all my people.'

"Lt. Herrick came back, and he didn't like that old boy either. When he heard what was happening, he was about to fistfight the guy right there. But the battalion commander came running up and demanded, 'What's wrong?' Herrick told him, 'This eight ball was accusing my men of being cowards. There's no boats and no bridge for them to cross on, and they were taking casualties, so Sgt. Hansen pulled them back.'

"The battalion commander said, 'I don't see nothin' wrong with that. You men just wait here, there'll be some boats here in a few minutes.'

"Soon a truck brought a big load of metal flat-bottomed boats. Each squad grabbed one and we headed down to the river again. We threw the front end of the boat into the water and I jumped in first. The river was 200 yards wide; a dam had been blown upstream, and all that water was hitting us. It flowed so fast it pulled the boat out of our hands. There goes the boat and I'm the only man in it. I jumped in the river and made it back to shore somehow.

"We ran back up and got another boat, put it in the water, and all of a sudden here comes a mortar shell. The sound of those will cause you to freeze. So we just froze. The shell punched right through the bottom of the boat but fortunately didn't explode.

"So there we were on our third boat. Our men had put up a smokescreen over the river to keep the Germans from observing how accurate their artillery was. We couldn't see from one side of the river to the other. We paddled out into that river, and the boat started spinning around and around, completely disorienting us.

"We finally made it to shore. I jumped off and grabbed the front of the boat and held it while everybody else got off. I said, 'Let's get the hell away from this river.' We let the boat go and took off running. The platoon's objective happened to be three buildings to the right of where we crossed the river. Through the smoke to my right, I recognized three buildings. So I spread the men out in fighting formation and said, 'We're going after them right now.' We moved about 50 feet and then we saw Americans going the other direction!

"One of my men said, 'Sergeant, we better get our butts back to the river, they're withdrawing!'

"I said, 'Withdrawing hell. We're on the same side of the river where we started!'"

"No way," I said.

"On the fourth attempt, we made it across the river and immediately ran into a minefield. I happened to be the one in front, so I got to lead them through it. I told them to follow in my footsteps. The riverbed had been flooded for so long it was nothing but mud, and I felt sure I could see the wire prongs of those antipersonnel mines. It was just a little round metal ball with three wire prongs, and if you stepped on a prong it would explode.

"We made it through the minefield, and the Germans started shooting at us from those three buildings we were supposed to take. They hit two of our men right off.

"I told the men, 'Whenever they shoot one round at you, you send fifty back towards them.' We fired back, drove them into the woods, and took off running toward them. Inside the woods, the battle got really hot. We got in close and shot at each other from behind trees. I loaded up my weapon with armor-piercing ammunition, and with that I could shoot right through the tree trunks.

"Suddenly the Germans vanished from the face of the Earth. We couldn't tell where they went. Finally a white flag came up out of the ground and waved back and forth.

"I told all my men to hide. A German soldier approached us with that white flag, really waving it so nobody would shoot him. An officer came up out of the ground behind him. I edged closer. He saluted and I saluted him.

"He looked me over and said, 'What rank are you?' He spoke perfect English. I said, 'I'm a general.'

"He grinned and asked, 'How many men have you got?'

"I said, 'I have enough. Listen fella, if you're here to surrender, fine, let's get on with the surrender, but if you're just gonna ask questions, the war's fixin' to crank up again.'

"He said, 'I have wounded soldiers. Will they be taken care of?' I said, 'They will if you surrender, but if you don't, they'll have to take their chances along with the rest.'

"He said, 'I'm going to talk to my men. It will take ten minutes.' I said, 'I'll give you five minutes. If you're not back here in five minutes we'll start shooting.'

"He went into three dugouts and a small building, and in about three minutes he came back and said, 'They're all going to come out and surrender.'

"All their men who weren't wounded came out and piled up their weapons and got into formation. We went into the dugouts to look for more weapons and found fifteen wounded. I asked the officer for one soldier who spoke English, and I gave the white flag to that man and told him to stay there with the wounded, and I would try to find some medics to help them.

"I told the officer, 'I'm not going back through that minefield. We'll go up to Tetz.' That was a little town about a quarter of a mile away.

"So he marched his men into Tetz for us." He laughed. "I was always envious watching the German soldiers march. They could march in perfect unison, and we never could no matter how hard we tried.

"We got into Tetz and I couldn't see a soul. I thought to myself, 'Uh-oh, something's wrong here. In a few minutes either they'll still be our prisoners or we'll be theirs, I don't know which way it's gonna go.'

"All of a sudden our battalion commander stepped out of a building. He saw the Germans, jumped back inside, looked out again, and said, 'Hansen, where in the hell did you get *them?*'

"I told him they were defending our objective. I told him we had a little trouble getting across the river and I was down to sixteen men. I didn't know where my officer or the rest of the platoon was, hadn't seen them since we started to cross the river.

"I asked him, 'Do you know where F Company is?' He grinned and said, 'They're up on this hill right ahead of us, pinned down up there. Would you like to join them?' I said, 'Not really.'

"By now they had a bridge built across the river, and the quartermaster was carrying ammunition across. Trucks carried ammo into Tetz. We loaded up with ammo and took some extra for the other men and headed up the hill. Halfway up I met the company commander, who told me, 'We're taking a lot of fire from our right. See what you can do about it.'

"I took my men back down the hill, and we circled around and came up to a valley between two hills. The Germans were on top of one, and F Company was on top of the other. We crawled up the one with the Germans until we were right below them, and then we stood up and opened fire. Some of them surrendered; others just ran.

"I decided not to pursue them because we were getting too spread out. We returned to the valley, and here came a German Red Cross flag. Medics were coming after their wounded. So we respected that and let them do it, which was more than the Germans did sometimes.

"But they made a mistake. They picked up what we thought were wounded and started carrying them back, and just before they got out of sight one man jumped off the stretcher and started running. We said, 'Uh-oh! That's not wounded they're carrying.' They used the medics to help combat-capable men escape. So we started shooting. The medics were fair game at that point too.

"The Germans counterattacked with tanks and infantry that night. Our artillery pinned their infantry down before they ever got to us, but the tanks kept coming. There's not much you can do with tanks at night. The Germans get buttoned up inside those things, and you can't get to them. But we did manage to knock a few tracks off, and when the tracks came off they surrendered."

"How'd you do it?"

"We found a post or anything we could stick into the track when they put their brake on to turn. That would stretch the tread out and pop it off.

"I got wounded as we tried to capture Beeck, Germany. We'd already failed in two previous attempts to take it and had to withdraw back down a hill for the second time to get more ammunition and replacements. We decided to make one more try and entered an orchard, where we got stopped again. The Germans were only 200 yards away, and they could see everything we did. There was no surprise in our attacks at all.

"The captain told me, 'We're going to attack again in two hours. In one hour and 15 minutes we're going to lambaste that town with artillery.' So I climbed back up the hill, got almost to the crest, and knelt down and rested a minute in the mud and rain. I peeked over the crest to find my foxhole and noticed deep tank tracks running right past it. So I thought to myself 'I'll run alongside that tank track, and if somebody shoots at me I'll just dive into the track.'

"I took off running as hard as I could, and all of a sudden there was the most terrific explosion I ever heard. It knocked me backwards. My subconscious mind was still working, saying, 'Tank track! Tank track!' Then I faded out, and when I regained consciousness I felt something tugging on my back. I had a combat pack holding my mess kit and everything else. Then I felt the tug again, and I realized it was a bullet going through my backpack, which was sticking up above the edge of the tank track.

"I hollered, 'Hembre, get him off my back!' Hembre was my foxhole buddy at that time.

"He said, 'I can't find him!'

"I said, 'Well, he's out there somewhere.'

"A little haystack stood across the valley in front of G Company. Those guys decided to load up with tracer ammunition and shoot into that stack to see if they could light it. Sure enough, it caught on fire. Turned out the German shooter was hiding in a foxhole dug beneath that haystack. When the fire got to him, he came running out of there, but he didn't get far. Not only was G Company shooting at him, F Company was too. I jumped up out of the track and ran and jumped into my hole with Hembre. He opened my first aid pack and put a bandage around my head.

"A medic came crawling up that tank track and joined us. After dark he got me out of there and down to the first aid station. They put me on an ambulance and took me to a clearing hospital. Everything was blacked out. Inside there, the medic took the bandage off my head and said, 'Well, that's not gonna be too bad.'

"I was supposed to stay at the hospital for several days to recover, but I got fed up with it. I wanted to be back with my unit, so I just up and left. After I'd been back at the front line for a while, one of my commanders saw me and asked, 'What the hell are you trying to pull? The hospital just called and said you left without permission.'

"I said, 'Tell them I'm on the way.' And I walked out and went back to my platoon.

"Of course, I've been paying for that ever since. I've had ringing in my ears. And when I filed for compensation, they found out I'd been AWOL, so I had to explain to them that I had gone back to my platoon, didn't want to leave my boys alone. They finally gave me a little compensation.

"From the Ruhr to the Rhine was about 35 miles, and getting across that 35 miles was pure hell. But the men kept their sense of humor. They were all gamblers. If one of our soldiers got caught out in the open with German snipers shooting at him, our boys would place bets on whether he'd make it or not!

"We took a bunch of small towns on the way to the Rhine. During the battle for Krefeld in February 1945 I got a battlefield commission and became a second lieutenant.

"At Krefeld some of us got relieved because we hadn't had any rest since we went into combat. We were pretty raunchy; we hadn't had a shower in almost two months. All we'd been able to do was fill our helmets with water and take towel baths.

"While we rested behind the front, a German dog took up with me. Everywhere I'd go she'd go right with me. Turned out she was pregnant. She was so attached to me that nobody dared mess with me. If I stopped she'd sit right alongside of me, lean up against my leg, and look up at me. One night she had eight puppies, so I started putting an extra man on my ration requests to get food for her. I'm a sucker for animals.

"I rummaged through some bombed-out houses and found a cross on a ribbon. Judging by the weight, I guessed it was solid silver. I found two young German ladies who spoke English and asked them what it meant. One of them smiled and said, 'That is a sterling silver cross that Hitler gave a mother who had six or more children.'

"I thought, 'My dog had eight puppies, so she deserves a medal!' I put it around her neck, and we went for a walk. We headed down a sidewalk and passed a group of about twenty women conversing across the road. They noticed the dog and got highly indignant. Having that cross around her neck was an insult to their motherhood. They started chasing her! Of course the durn dog ran right to me, so I took off too. I ran back to headquarters, grabbed my pistol, came back out, and fired three rounds into the air. The women dispersed.

"A couple mornings later Sgt. Smith from 2nd Platoon came over and held a formation with 1st Platoon. He called me out and read a citation he'd written up: 'By order of someone, Lt. Hansen is hereby cited for single-handedly breaking up a huge ugly mob of thugs bent on doing harm. In spite of the type of people making up the mob (old women and little children) Lt. Hansen showed no fear. For this heroic action Lt. Hansen is awarded the Barbed Wire Cluster with a Double Cross Medal.' It said the medal would be forthcoming, but I never did get it.

"When the Americans crossed the Rhine, those of us in Krefeld faked the Germans out. We acted like we intended to cross the Rhine right there, so the Germans built up their forces across the river from us. We were one division pretending to be three. We had rubber artillery pieces, rubber tanks, camouflage, and the Germans really thought we had a big buildup there. But the real river crossing took place at Wesel, north of us, and the Germans weren't expecting that.

"After we crossed the river, the chase was on and we headed for the Elbe River. We moved carefully through the woods toward Gardelegen. And that's where we saw them."

"Saw who?" I asked.

"I had one scout up ahead of us to check things out as we walked through these woods. He whistled at me and gestured for me to come up and talk to him. He whispered, 'I don't know what that is lying there by that tree. I think it's a zebra.'

182

"I took a look and said, 'I think that's a *human*.'

"We dodged from tree to tree and made our way up there. Sure enough it was a man lying there, but he was so thin he barely seemed human. He wore a black and white striped prisoner's outfit. He could barely lift his hand.

"He whispered to us in English that he wanted water and food. So I poured some water in his mouth. I opened up some K-rations and gave him a bite of a cracker. He ate a little bit of it, and then he just died right there in front of us. He'd been without food for so many days, his system couldn't handle it. But we didn't understand what had happened.

"We moved deeper into the woods and found more of them lying around, too thin and weak to get up and move. We fed a little bit to another man and the same thing happened again. We lost a few before we realized food was too much of a shock to their system after starving for so long. We quit giving them food and water and called in the medics. Then we moved on.

"I looked into Gardelegen and saw smoke coming up from the left side of town. I thought maybe the Germans had fired an ammunition dump. We followed the smoke and found a barn with smoke coming out the doors on either side.

"I walked around on one side of the barn, and the rest of the platoon went around on the other. I came across a long trench and saw bodies lined up in the bottom, some half-covered with dirt, others just lying in the open.

"The men on the other side of the barn screamed at me. I ran to them. They had opened one of the doors, revealing a mass of bodies covering the floor of the barn, all burned.

"The Germans had marched a group of political prisoners into Gardelegen. That was as far as they could take them because we were catching up. So they put straw on the floor of the barn and doused it with gasoline. They put the prisoners in there, telling them they could sleep on straw that night. The prisoners hurried into the barn to find a comfortable place to sleep. By the time they smelled the gasoline, it was too late. The Germans closed the doors and ignited the gas and straw with phosphorus grenades. We would later count a total of 1,016 bodies in the barn and in the mass grave outside.

"We didn't know it at the time, but seven political prisoners who had escaped the fire were hiding in nearby woods when we arrived. As we surveyed the horrible scene, two German Red Cross members, a man and a woman, approached a group of our officers and asked if they could be of assistance. Of course the German Red Cross was not like our own Red Cross; it was an apparatus of the Nazi government.

"As our officers talked with these two Germans, one of the survivors emerged from the woods and walked calmly and quietly up to the group. He could have been French, Dutch, Polish, Hungarian, or from any of the other countries Germany invaded. I'm not sure because he never said a word. Without warning he grabbed a pistol from an American officer's holster and fired point blank at the two Germans. It happened so fast, nobody was able to stop him."

"What did you do to him afterwards?" I asked.

"Nothing. He wandered off and nobody tried to detain him. Nobody wanted to. What could we do? The charred bodies of his countrymen were lying all over the place.

"Our division made the German townspeople dig up all the people who'd been buried or partially buried in the trench. We also cleared a path through the bodies in the barn from one door to the other, and we forced the entire population of this town, at gunpoint, to walk through the barn and witness what had been done."

"How did they react?" I asked.

"Some fainted, some got sick. Some tried to refuse to enter, but our men forced them to go. If they wouldn't walk through they got carried through. And they couldn't turn back; they had to go all the way from one end to the other.

"Then, after our engineers laid out a military cemetery, we made them dig individual graves and give all the bodies a proper burial. I visited there two years ago, and they have made a beautiful cemetery out of that. The people of Gardelegen maintain it to this day."

"Were you totally unprepared for this, or had you heard stories by then?" I asked.

"We had heard about Buchenwald already."

"But how did you handle actually seeing this with your own eyes?"

"When you're in combat for so long a time," Jim Hansen said, "you're not yourself. You're really on the level of an animal. And that's the way it's got to be. If you had any common sense about you in combat, you'd go crazy. When they get you reduced to the level of an animal, that's when you make a good soldier. Because of that I was able to handle this. The training was so tough we were ready for anything."

"You've never suffered any flashbacks or anything like that?"

"One thing happened a few years back: Our house got hit by lightning in the middle of the night. I was sound asleep and it sounded exactly like an artillery shell hitting. I immediately reached for my gun in the darkness. All I got was a computer mouse."

Jim Hansen went back to visit Gardelegen in 2000. Here he meets with the lady mayor of Gardelegen and the board chairman of the cemetery where the burning victims are buried.

Jim Hansen with his wife, Bonnie, around 1995.

There were no visible tears...
We just made the best of it

Sally Mitchell
Comfort

"**I** married Robert in December of '39," Sally Mitchell told me, "when he was stationed at Fort Sam Houston in San Antonio. He went to Ft. Leavenworth to attend some training in 1941. He was on the golf course there when he heard about Pearl Harbor, and I was staying with my mother.

"He served in field artillery as an instructor. He was sent to many bases during the war—Camp Hood, Camp Bowie, Camp Polk in Louisiana, Fort Sill in Oklahoma. Sometimes I'd go with him, and sometimes I'd stay with my mother. All during the war I was having children, and Robert was never around when they were born! I had four during the war and a fifth in 1946.

"I also had four brothers, and they all went into the service. Gorham, George, Vinton, and Charles."

"Did they all come back?"

"Yes, they all came back. My husband didn't go overseas; every time he was about to go they'd ship him off to another training camp to train soldiers. I'd go with him to these little towns, and we'd have to find a place to live. We

Maj. Robert Mitchell home on leave with Sally in 1943.

lived in very modest rooms, nothing luxurious. People in all the towns were remodeling their garages and barns and little shacks and renting them out to the military families."

"How did it go when you stayed with your mom?"

She laughed. "I'm sure there were times my mother could have killed me and all my children too, but we had a good relationship.

"We had quite a few men in our neighborhood go to war, but only one was killed. John Brinkmeyer. Our families were friends. In those days the families in a neighborhood were all friendly with each other, like one big family. It's not like that any more."

"What did your brothers do in the service?"

"Charles went to Europe, Gorham went to New Guinea, Vinton went to the Philippines, and George went to Australia. They went into the service one at a time as they were drafted.

"We didn't know anything about when they would be shipped out, of course. That was all kept secret. When Charles, the youngest, left, he was staying with us while he was stationed at Fort Sam Houston, and he went to the base one day and didn't come back. He had told my mother that some day he'd be shipped out; he couldn't tell her when, but when he didn't come home that day, she'd know he was gone. People were a lot better at keeping secrets those days."

"How did you react when he didn't come back that day?"

"We just said, 'Well, Charlie's gone.' There were no visible tears, and there may not have been any in private either. This was war and that was the way it was. We were

Sally Mitchell's four brothers in 1940, while they were in college.
From left, George, Gorham, Charles, and Vinton Hartwell.

all in it together and we just made the best of it. We talked about them while they were gone, wondered what they were doing. We'd get letters with what little they could tell us. Any information about their location was off limits. But we were just glad to know they were all right."

"How often did you get mail?"

"It would come in spurts. We'd get a whole bunch at once and then we'd get none for a while. It was a happy day when we got mail.

"My father put together a book of memoirs called *Pop's Weekly*. He wrote a letter every week to all his boys and to the boys from the neighborhood. He also gathered up letters from the other families and assembled them in the weekly and mailed a copy of it to each one of those boys every week like clockwork. It turned out to be quite a thing, always full of encouraging messages from the neighborhood to the boys.

```
                                        San Antonio, Texas, Nov. 26th 1944.

Dear Boys:-

        Well we have reason this week to feel the spirit of
Thanksgiving as the mailman was kind to us, leaving one letter from
Gorham, one from Charles Milby and anmfxam two from George, besides
one from Max and one from Billy Brinkmeyer, and all reported being in
good health etc.  In addition the news from all fronts continues
good with indications that we have gone over the hump and are rolling
down grade in with increasing speed to Victoria a nd PEACE. Kxikafxkixx
PEACE. that wonderful condition of life which we all most want and
which we hope will obtain for many years to come.  We had another wet
da-y yesterday (Friday) but last thisafternoon (Saturday), it has
cleared and is beautiful with a good north wind so I presume we are
in for a little cold weather, and the pacans are raining down.

              Now for the mail.
From GorhamX!-Nov. 13th 1944.  Dear Folks:- I haven't written very much
lately, beca use there is so darned little to write a-bout.   Ma-il
hasn't been coming in very good lately.  The last letter I gor from
George was Sept. 17th, and quite a while since I have had any from
home.  I guess they will be coming along soon.  I would like to
knowhow everything back there is going.  I guess you have gotten word
about my promotion.  I have had it since Sept. 17th but didn't find
out about it till la-te in October.  I still haven't gotten used to
First instead of Sexdnd Lt.    Give my love to everyone,        Gorham.

Well GoGo as aixnaxs always we were gaii glad to hear from you and to
know that you are well etc.  The length of the letter does not count
so much as knowing that you are safe and well.  Write when it is con-
venient.  We would be interested in some of the little things that come
up with you in spite of the X fact that we may not know the persons to
whom you refer.  And dont get discouraged about mail it will come
a-long.   Poor McRae Hill kept eriting that he had not received ahy
mail from home at all, then one day he got 35 letters.  Dðnt you know
he was a busy lieutenant for some time.  We are still happy over your
promotion, but I am also ynhappy about its long delay inarriving.  I
dont suppose there is anything we can do about it though so lets go
on and be happy about it anyway.

From Charlie:- Oct. 21st 1944:-Dear Mom:- Thought you'd like to know
thatX I am still alive and kicking.  That is I would be kicking if I
could lift my feet high enough out of this mud.  To-day it rained
only half a day so we can classify that as a holiday.  It hasn't
been so cold la-tely so I am not so bad off.  I received a slug of
mail last week so I justabout up to snuff.  Mail seems to travel very
slow now.  I received a letter from Grace, which was well over a xm
month getting here.  Chow has improved quite a bðt herelately, but
I still think they should legalize axe murders in case a soldier's
wife serves him Spa-m ( or anything that looks or tastes like it),
powdered eggs, orange marmala-de, or meat and vegetable stew (C rations
```

A page from an issue of *Pop's Weekly,* a collection of letters from the neighborhood boys overseas and their supporters back home that Sally Mitchell's father compiled and distributed on a regular basis.

"He wasn't a very good typist, but he typed it up and he made hectograph copies. That's where you pour a special gel into a tray, coat the gel with glycerin, and place the original document on top of the gel. The glycerin reacts with the ink, transferring the image of the original into the gel. Then you lay a blank sheet of paper on the gel, and it transfers the ink back, creating a copy of the original. That's how he reproduced it. This was way back before copying machines."

"How often did you write letters to your brothers?"

"I wrote a whole lot more than I do now. I wrote as often as I could, reporting the daily happenings in the neighborhood.

"The censors blacked out certain things. Most of the boys learned what they couldn't talk about, but sometimes they would have something in there that let you know where they were, and that got blacked out. One time my brother George in Australia sent us a letter, and it had some things blacked out on it, but he had also sent some pictures. In one picture was a pile of trash, and in that pile there was a sign that said Townsville. So we knew he was in Townsville, Australia. The censors let that one get by them.

"Gorham served in the infantry in New Guinea and was wounded and went to the hospital in Biak. George found out where he was and traveled up from Australia to see him. That was a great day for them, and it was a great day for us when we found out they'd seen each other."

"Tell me some ways in which your daily life was affected by the war," I said.

Sally Mitchell's parents hung this blue star banner in their window
during the war to indicate five family members serving in the military.

"The big one was, most of the time we didn't have our
husbands with us and were raising our children alone. I
was lucky; at least I got to see my husband on weekends.

"Communication is much easier now. We didn't have as
many ways to get in touch with people. But that was all we
knew. We wrote letters. We didn't use the telephone all the
time like we do now.

"We had to live with rationing, which, by the way, I don't think hurt anybody. We never did without anything we really needed. Gasoline, sugar, Crisco, Wesson oil, things like that were hard to get. But we never thought about what we couldn't get. We got along with what had. Fortunately my parents didn't have a car so they didn't have to worry about getting gasoline.

"I remember we used to save the tinfoil from cigarette packs and chewing gum wrappers, until they started making them without it. When the Lucky Strike packages

A family gathering at Christmas 1943, while all the boys were overseas.

changed from green to white, the saying was 'Lucky Strike Green has gone to war.'"

"How did you spend your time?"

"Raising all those children! For entertainment, we would go to each other's houses for lunch. People visited each other much more than they do now. Aside from visiting, raising children and taking care of the house took up a lot of time."

"How hard was it, raising so many children?" I asked. I have one child and sometimes I wonder how anybody could possibly handle two.

1944   JUNE   1944

S.	M.	T.	W.	T.	F.	S.
					1	2	3
4	5	6	7	8	9	10
11	12	13	14	15	16	17
18	19	20	21	22	23	24
25	26	27	28	29	30	

SUNDAY LIG
SAN ANTONIO

AN INDEPENDENT   TEXAS   NEWSPA

VOL. LXIV—NO. 158.   SUNDAY, JUNE 25, 1944.

TRIPLE THREAT TO FOE

Triplets and a fourth brother serve in this San Antonio family. Lieut. C. M. Hartwell (extreme left), now serving in England, is shown with the triplets (left to right): Lieut. Gorham G. Hartwell, with the infantry in New Guinea; Sgt. George H. Hartwell, air corps, stationed in Australia, and Lieut. Vinton James Hartwell, coast artillery, at Fort Moultrie, S. C. They are the sons of Mr. and Mrs. G. H. Hartwell, whose residence is at 111 East Courtland place.

Sally Mitchell's brothers appeared together in the *San Antonio Light* on June 25, 1944.

"I don't think raising kids was nearly as hard then as it is now," she said. "Sure, it could be tedious, the same thing over and over. Mothers got very tired in those days, but that was our job. And it was a job we very much wanted.

"We didn't have these thousands of books on child rearing; we just used our good common sense. It's hard for me to keep quiet when I hear my grandchildren talk about 'This book says to do this, this book says to do that'—I want to tell them, 'Just use your head and a lot of love!'

"These days most mothers work outside the home, so their children spend a lot of time in day care. Parents don't watch their children growing moment by moment; they don't have the closeness they used to. I think because of that closeness the children grew up respecting their parents and other adults more in those days.

"Today young people think they know everything. They don't want to be told what to do or how to do it. But the world is in pretty bad shape in my opinion. In those days we could go almost anywhere we wanted to, day or night. Today, in many places, people won't even venture out in the daytime.

"Children used to be brought up to respect their elders. Now they talk back to adults pretty bad. Sometimes it's pretty hard for me to keep my mouth shut!" she chuckled.

"Neighborhoods worked a lot differently then. Now it's almost as if your house is a place to hide from everything. When I was growing up, our next-door neighbors were sort of like second parents. We could go in and out of each other's houses, and we were always there for each other if we were needed. We knew everybody for two blocks around in all directions, and they knew us. And if we kids were doing something we weren't supposed to, our mothers and fathers would find out. Other adults could reprimand us just like our own mother and father could."

There's an idea for a fun experiment, I thought. Next time you see some of the neighborhood kids getting into trouble, try disciplining them as if they were your own.

"You know, I never hired a babysitter until my oldest boy was eleven or twelve. Didn't need one. We didn't take our kids as many places. We didn't *go* as many places, didn't do as much. But if we did go out, we'd have somebody in the family watch them. I didn't have anybody who wasn't a relative watch my kids until they were pretty big boys.

"Another thing that's changed," she continued, "is the way families eat dinner. Back then we always had meals together. That ties a family together. Now the kids run into the kitchen, grab some bread and butter, and run off to do whatever they want. Everyone in the family is going off in their own direction. There's few times when the entire family is all in one place.

"The kids didn't have as many clothes as kids have now, and the clothes weren't as cute, but we had enough of what we needed. We had plenty of diapers, but we had to do a lot of diaper washing."

I imagined what it would be like to use cloth diapers and have to wash and reuse them. Disposable diapers, I decided, go right along with air conditioning on my list of Modern Comforts I Cannot Do Without.

"From time to time I'd get frustrated and think, 'All I do is get up, fix breakfast, wash dishes, make the beds, fix lunch, wash dishes, then it's time for supper.' I never had any quiet time when the kids were little.

"The radio was on all the time. I listened to Jack Benny, Bing Crosby, Fibber McGee and Molly. Sometimes they had good dance music programs on, and all the neighborhood friends would meet at somebody's house, roll the carpets up, and dance.

"Other times women would get together and sew. We'd sit around, have lunch, knit or do embroidery, and visit with each other."

"How aware were your children of the war?"

"I think the oldest one and maybe the second one might have been aware. Oldest one, born in 1940, knew quite a bit I think. The others knew their daddy and uncles were off somewhere, but I doubt they understood what was going on. They couldn't see it on TV. We didn't have it."

"What do you remember about your brothers coming home?" I asked.

"We were living on a farm out from Camp Hood. We didn't have a telephone, so to make a call we had to go into town. My brother Charlie had left Germany and was on his way to the Pacific. It looked like he would have to fight in both theaters. His ship made it almost to the Panama Canal and then the war ended, so it turned around and came back to the States.

"My mother was visiting with me, and we went to town to call my father. He made some vague, teasing reference to Charlie, and I *knew*. I said 'Mama, Charlie's coming home!' So we got in the car right away and made the two-and-a-half-hour drive down to San Antonio. And he was there. He returned the same way he left—unannounced. He just walked back into the house.

"Charlie went through some rough days over there in Europe. Gorham, who went to New Guinea, had some really rough days too. George served as an aircraft mechanic in Australia, fixing damaged planes, so his service wasn't too bad. Vinton was in the States during most of the war and went to the Philippines just before the war ended."

"Were they able to adjust to civilian life easily after the war?"

"All except Gorham, who'd been through the roughest time, fighting those jungle battles out in the Pacific. He still doesn't like to talk about it. He hasn't told us much at all about what happened. But all my brothers had careers and did very well for themselves over the years.

"My husband stayed in the service and fought in the Korean War. After the Korean War I met him in Japan, and we lived there for a while. He retired in 1959."

"How did you like being a military wife?" I asked.

"I didn't like moving around all the time because of the children," she said. "Children need stability. But I did enjoy getting to see the different places we went.

"Truth is, I wasn't a very good Army wife because I didn't pay much attention to the social aspects, like playing bridge. I didn't like to play bridge. Thank goodness Robert didn't make me. I was more interested in spending time with my children, watching them grow up."

Sally Mitchell today.

I wanted to go off to war, and
my mother wouldn't let me

William White
Spring Branch

"I lived with my mother and stepfather out north of El Paso in an area called Kern Place, right at the edge," William White told me. "There wasn't anything north of us except desert. So I grew up out in the country climbing mountains and hunting jackrabbits.

"The senior class had just gotten back from a trip to Mexico City. Our high school played a football game against a Mexican high school, Mexico City Polytechnic Institute. This was the first American-style football game a Mexican high school had ever played. A special train took us down to Mexico City as special guests of the Mexican president. It was quite a trip; the train carried a carload of Mexican infantrymen to keep the bandits away from us as we passed through an area south of Chihuahua. A lot of bandits attacked trains down there in those days.

"About a week after we got back to El Paso, a bunch of us were at the movies with our dates when they interrupted the show to announce Pearl Harbor had been bombed.

"I had some friends who were a semester ahead of me in high school; I was seventeen and they were eighteen,

William White in 1945.

and they graduated that January. All three of them immediately joined the Marine Corps. I decided that was what I wanted to do, too. And my mother and stepfather informed me that no, in fact that was *not* what I wanted to do. Everybody who knows me kids me about the fact that I wanted to go off and fight a war but my mother wouldn't let me!"

"Did they just want to make sure you graduated from high school first?"

"More than that. I had committed to Texas A&M. They wanted me to go down there and at least give a shot at my degree. So I went to A&M, thinking I was well protected from the draft because they weren't drafting anyone below twenty-one at that time. Then in September of 1942 they changed the draft age to eighteen, and I knew I'd get caught up in that. You didn't get an exemption if you were in a military school unless you were already a junior or senior. So I volunteered for the Navy in December of 1942."

"What did your parents think?"

"They didn't have much of a choice, because I was certainly subject to the draft. I didn't want to be drafted. I wanted to volunteer. Everybody I knew wanted to volunteer.

"I arrived by train in San Diego at three o'clock in the morning and experienced quite a culture shock. As a freshman at A&M I had experienced a disciplined environment, but not to the degree that I was confronted with in boot camp. I thought I was in pretty good shape, but I wasn't.

"We had run obstacle courses at A&M but nothing like what we ran in San Diego. These courses were a mile and a half long. We did calisthenics forever. Every spare moment we had to do some exercise. They didn't give us much chance to be homesick in those days; they occupied every moment of our time. We were tired when we went to bed, and we had to get up at 4:30 in the morning. At least we had good food.

"That lasted from December to February. They gave us a battery of written and oral exams to determine our qualification. They chose me for sonar school; they called it sound school then. It was in San Diego. I went there for two months then joined my ship."

"What was sound school like?" I asked.

"Rigorous. They kept us busy; everything was crammed into short periods of time. I guess they figured if they threw enough mud at us, some of it would stick. It kept my brain busy.

"We got our sea practice on Eagle Boats, old World War I submarine chasers built by Ford Motor Co. They were top-heavy as the devil, and if you didn't get seasick on those, you probably never would.

"They taught us all about the dome that emitted the sound waves. We learned to discern whether a submarine was coming toward us or going away by the sound of the echo."

"How does that work?"

"If the submarine is headed toward you, the echo comes back at a higher frequency than the sound that went out. If the echo is lower, in other words the cycles are farther apart, the submarine is headed away. And you can usually distinguish a submarine from a whale by the way it moves. A submarine can't maneuver as quickly as a whale or a school of fish. But sometimes it was hard to tell. The ship's crew would get pretty ticked off at you if you had them all called to general quarters in the middle of the night to put down ash cans on a school of fish or a whale!"

"Did you ever have false alarms like that?"

"On occasion. Once or twice I couldn't tell them apart. Fish can make all kinds of noises that will cause a sonar man trouble. Porpoises make a heck of a racket. One type of fish, croakers, ran in schools and absolutely ruined the operation of the sonar. They made a noise that sounded like a machine gun."

"How did they do that?"

"Don't ask me."

"What ship did you join after sound school?"

"I was assigned to a patrol craft, PC-1127, a steel-hulled submarine chaser. It was built in Michigan and floated down the Ohio and Mississippi Rivers to New Orleans, where it was commissioned in May of 1943. It was 175 feet long and 27 feet wide and had sixty men and five officers. Later we also took on five frogmen when we joined the amphibious corps.

"Before leaving New Orleans, the biggest body of water I'd ever seen was Elephant Butte Lake up in New Mexico. Now we crossed the Gulf of Mexico and attended several weeks of anti-submarine training in Miami. The Navy had taken over several hotels and brought in a bunch of sailors, including Russian and English ones, to learn anti-submarine warfare.

"In the Atlantic outside Miami, we had our only encounter with a German U-boat. The Germans had developed a chemical device that would form a pocket of millions of air bubbles when it came in contact with saltwater. They called this thing a *pillenwerfer*. When they shot it out of its

PC-1127 covered with ice in Bay City, Michigan, before it traveled downriver to New Orleans for commissioning in May 1943. PC-1126 and 1128 are also visible in the background.

launcher, the big air pocket would create a signature on our sonar that closely resembled a submarine. We'd get a sonar reading on the air pocket instead of the submarine, and it lasted just long enough for the sub to get away. At the time I thought the U-boat was dead in the water or stopped, but about ten minutes later we figured out we were echo sounding on an air pocket. By then the submarine was gone.

PC-1127's officers.

"We stopped at Key West on the way to the Panama Canal and went into a dry-dock for a day or so. There I got promoted to sonarman second class.

"Before we put the ship in dry-dock, we had retracted the ship's sonar dome into the hull. Once we were back in the water, we needed to lower it beneath the hull again. The job fell to me, even though I had no idea what I was doing.

"We hadn't started the ship's generators yet, which meant no electricity. I had to lower the dome manually. I was down in the lower sound room with a pair of headphones on, letting the skipper, Byron Voegelin, know the progress of my efforts. I had failed to put the brake on, and I lost the sonar dome and the shaft. It dropped down through the water to the bottom of the ocean.

"Once it hit bottom it was ruined; its interior was a delicate maze of quartz crystals that couldn't stand an impact like that. It cost thousands of dollars, too.

"I didn't say anything for a while, so the skipper asked me what was going on. I said, 'I'd better come up and tell you face to face.' It was particularly hard to tell this to him because he'd just promoted me."

"Uh-oh," I said. "What did he do?"

"He just grunted and grumbled a little. I'm sure he thought to himself, 'We'll never be able to do anything with these civilian sailors.' But he never said anything to me.

"We passed through the Panama Canal and pulled into a little Mexican port called Salina Cruz, south of Acapulco. No other U.S. Navy ship had ever been in that port. But there was not a thing in that town we could pay for. The town just closed down and welcomed us for the two days we were there. It was amazing. They held a fiesta for us. We ate a lot. They fed us a lot of fish, a lot of shrimp.

"Whenever we walked by the army constabulary in town, it didn't make any difference what rank we were, the two Mexican sentries out front brought their rifles up and presented arms to us! They wanted us to know they supported us. It was quite an experience for an eighteen-year-old kid.

"We refueled there and then joined the 2nd Marine Division at Pearl Harbor. In November we headed south without knowing where we were going.

"The skipper told us through the loudspeaker we were going to a place in the Gilbert Islands called Betio, in the Tarawa Atoll. That was to be the site of our first conflict. We'd never heard of it."

Tarawa (pronounced Tuh-RAW-uh) was where the United States tested its ability to land on and capture a heavily defended beach in preparation for the long campaign of island hopping across the Pacific. The largest island, Betio, is one square mile in size. More than 1,000 Americans died in the battle.

"The skipper told us the Japanese resistance would be tough, but the fleet was already there, pounding the island with shells. Our ship would serve as a landing craft control vessel. We would escort LSTs to the landing zone.

"We moved in past the ships of the main fleet several thousand yards off shore. They'd been bombarding the island for several days. I've heard an estimate that they unleashed a thousand pounds of explosives per square foot on that island.

"We moved to a particular point along the beach, and the landing craft came up even with us at the line of departure. When we got the word from the command vessel several miles away, we signaled with pennants for the landing craft to head into the beach. We communicated between the beach control officer and the command vessel to pass along the status of the landing parties."

"Where were you on the ship during the battle?"

"I was always up in the pilot house, where the sonar gear was. During general quarters I manned the engine room telegraph, which was also in the pilot house."

"How much of the atoll could you see?" I asked.

"Betio was the only island within eyesight. I could make out the tops of palm trees, and that was about it. It was just a tiny strip of land, not much on it, and we were about 1,500 yards from shore.

"The bombardment was constant. I'd never seen anything like that. Hearing those 16-inch shells pass overhead was pretty nerve-wracking. They sounded like a fast Volkswagen, and they were about the size of one, too. We watched them hit.

"The landings didn't go smoothly. We lost a great number of men whose landing craft got hung up on the coral reef surrounding the island. Confusion took hold. But we didn't know what to do about it; we had to stay at our position. Then some landing craft came up from behind us and went in to try to rescue the men who'd been stranded out there.

"At that time we didn't have the fancier tractors we used in later invasions. The front of them didn't come down. The later models could go right up on the beach. The vehicles we used at Tarawa didn't have enough power to back up off the coral reef if they got hung up.

"When the tractors got hung up on the reef, we watched men climb out of them into the water, hold their rifles above their heads, and wade in toward shore. That was a disconcerting sight to say the least.

"We went ashore after the battle. The thing that stands out more than anything to me is the odor of dead men. I'll never forget that. By the time we got there they'd buried most of the bodies, but some still floated just off shore. I saw one of them.

"I walked around through absolute devastation. In the middle of the island I saw a particularly large reinforced concrete pillbox. The Japanese had dug in there, but the bombardment had busted it open.

"We joined the fighting at Bougainville, where the Japanese still held most of the island, but the Americans held a five-mile strip of land with three airfields off Empress Augusta Bay. We escorted PT boats to the mouth of a river near the southern tip of the island. At night the PTs went up the river to raise hell with Japanese emplacements on a ridge between the river and Bagana, a big volcano. We waited at the mouth of the river all night for them to return. We made sure no Japanese submarine got anywhere near them."

"Was this an active volcano?"

"Yes. It emitted smoke and steam the entire time we were there. In fact I may have kept an eye on that volcano even more than I did the Japanese!

"The Japanese wanted to evacuate some officers from the island. They would try to negotiate the river on rafts and meet their submarines at the mouth of the river. It was our job to make sure there were no Jap submarines waiting for them.

"The Japanese still held that area up there because the only thing on the island that really interested the Americans was the airstrips. The entire island of Bougainville was not an objective; it was just a stepping-stone. And building the three airfields there allowed our planes to attack Rabaul, the big Japanese naval base about 220 miles away.

"A destroyer joined us at the mouth of the river once, trying to do something about those Japanese gun emplacements, but it couldn't get close enough to the island to be accurate with their 5-inch guns. Since we had a smaller draft and could get closer in to shore, Voegelin had volunteered us to go up and knock them off that ridge. But I think the skipper lost interest when he realized the Japanese were shooting back at the destroyer up ahead of us!"

He chuckled. "Of course he'd already volunteered at that point, he didn't have any choice. We got within a mile of the ridge. The ship drew about 7 feet and we could get in pretty close to the riverbank. We had a 3-inch/50 forward on the bow, our longest-range weapon. We could see the ridge, maybe a mile, mile and a half away. We opened fire, and we had quite a crew on our gun. It took them only four or five shots to take out the emplacement.

"Did you come under fire?"

"Fortunately, no. I think they were too busy shooting at the destroyer to pay any attention to us.

"Another group used to go up the river—a bunch of Fijis who paddled up in canoes at night, armed only with machetes. They crept out into the jungle, caught the Japanese unaware, and killed them with machetes. They had no love for the Japanese. They looked meaner than snakes to me.

"Funny thing happened when we were anchored at Tulagi, which was across the Sabo Bay. Between Guadalcanal and Tulagi there's an island called Sabo. Later they called the bay Iron Bottom Sound because of all the ships that sank there during the war.

"Our ship had found an ideal berth, close to fresh water and close to the Navy post office that had been set up there. We had gone a long time without mail. We were the closest vessel to the beach. That was good, because being so small, the only way we had to get ashore was a little dory that held five people, and it was a wet ride. We weren't like the bigger ships that carried boats so big you could stand in them and not get wet.

"We'd been anchored there a day or two when a destroyer came up behind us and signaled. I was up on the flying bridge at that time; just about everybody else was off duty. I jumped up on the light and acknowledged them. It turned out they wanted us to move out of the way so they could take our berth!

"Bigger ships would sometimes bully smaller ships out of the best berths, you see. I took the message down to Voegelin in his wardroom, and he grunted and growled and wrote out a message. I went back up on the light and signaled that our skipper wanted the name, rank, and date of rank of their commanding officer.

"Of course I'm sure the destroyer crew thought since we were just a little PC, we didn't have much rank aboard. They signaled back that it was such and such lieutenant, U.S. Naval Reserve, 1940.

"Voegelin saw that and laughed and had me send back, 'Sorry, cannot comply. Signed, Lt. Commander Byron Voegelin, U.S. Navy, 1936.' So the destroyer backed off, and we all waved to it as it left!" He laughed gleefully.

"We returned to Pearl Harbor in spring of 1944 for modifications to the ship. We painted camouflage on our hull. We took on five frogmen and four Marine communications personnel. And we added so much communications equipment, the ship looked like a porcupine when we left the harbor.

"In Hawaii most of the crew got to spend a week at a Navy rest camp at Waianae on Oahu. We weren't used to that kind of treatment! We could order anything we wanted for breakfast. Didn't have to do anything. We had the beaches to ourselves. We didn't have surfboards, but we wet our mattress covers, filled them with air from the brisk breeze, tied the end in a knot, and made air mattresses. We rowed them out to 'catch a wave.' Boy, what a ride!

"And the Andrews Sisters put on a great show for 300 of us in an amphitheater. Those girls were tireless! They'd still be out there performing right now if they could, but we had to shut down about 2 a.m. They sang a lot of popular songs, including 'Rum and Coca-Cola' and 'I Can Dream, Can't I?'

"Radio equipment and seats were installed in the pilot-house for these Marine communications specialists to use. They added new bunks for them and the frogmen.

"These frogmen had the job of swimming up to the beach the night before a landing operation. We'd drop them off fairly close to shore and pick them up several hours later. They made sure no obstacles blocked the beach so the Marines could make a good landing. They had to clear out explosives and barricades. I wouldn't want that job, but they all seemed pretty enthusiastic about it. They were the forerunners of today's Navy SEALs.

"We went to Kwajalein. It was the fleet's embarkation point for the Marianas operation—Guam, Saipan, Tinian. We took on supplies there, and we knew we'd go into combat soon because we had fresh eggs and fresh fruit. That only happened when we were going into combat."

"What did you think about that?"

"All of us were anxious for that kind of thing. We were trained in combat and didn't want to just sit there. We were pleased that we'd be doing something. We didn't know *what* we'd be doing—they never told us anything until right before it happened."

"What was Kwajalein like?"

"It was one heck of a big atoll. I looked out across it, and I'd never seen so many ships in my life. The entire Fifth Fleet was there. Hundreds, possibly thousands of ships of all kinds: carriers, battlewagons, cruisers, and untold numbers of transports and tenders.

"One of the items brought aboard was Australian lamb, or mutton as we called it. And nobody in the United States Navy cared anything about mutton. The ships took it on because they were ordered to take it, but then they threw it overboard. And you could look out across the atoll and see big hunks of mutton floating everywhere." He laughed.

"We took our position close to some LSTs and then one morning the fleet got underway and headed west. We knew we were getting close to wherever we were going around the 16th of June, when six Japanese torpedo planes attacked us. I suppose they wanted to sink some landing ships, knowing thousands of men were aboard them.

"One made a run on the destroyer USS *Black*, our command vessel. We were just aft and starboard of the *Black*, and we saw the torpedo plane, a Kate, pass by close enough for us to see its two-man crew. When their torpedo bombers got ready to make a run, they got down close to the water and started to bob up and down. This one did just that, aiming straight for the *Black*. Then we blew him out of the air with our 3-inch/50-caliber gun. We always maintained the *Black* owed us their gratitude because they shot at him with everything they had. They just didn't have as good a shot as we did.

"During the air raid we lost communications with the 'talker' at the gun, and I went out there to tell him his telephone wasn't working. I got too close behind the gun, and a 3-inch/50 shell casing flew out and landed on my right foot, breaking the big toe.

"The other Japanese planes made torpedo runs on LSTs. I don't know if those pilots knew it beforehand, but attacking an LST from the air was suicidal. Those ships had 20mm guns, just one right after the other, on each side, and they could throw up one heck of a lot of lead. They shot the planes down.

"After we secured from general quarters the chief pharmacist's mate gave me what medical attention he could. He punctured the toenail with a needle to drain it and wrapped the toe to keep it immobile. I didn't miss any action because of it; on such a small ship, there's no room for anyone to be inactive for very long, and the injury wasn't severe enough for them to send me anywhere for medical attention. There was a hospital ship in the area, but they had room only for the gravely wounded, certainly not for something as minor as a broken toe. So I stayed on my ship and stayed on duty. I still have problems with that toe in wet or cold weather."

"How did you feel while watching this battle?" I asked.

"I was fascinated by the sight. I wasn't afraid at the time, but I was later! After it was all over, everybody was rattled. But in the middle of it, the adrenaline kicked in and kept us going.

"We were with the 1st and 3rd Marine divisions, which were scheduled to land on Guam on June 21, 1944. The 2nd and 4th Marines had already landed on Saipan on June

15. That invasion turned out to be more difficult than expected, so instead of landing on Guam we were held in reserve in case we were needed to reinforce the Saipan operation. We waited for word on whether we'd be needed, and it turned out we weren't. We'd been floating around out there since June 6, and that can be rough on ships like LSTs loaded full of men and little PCs. So on July 5th we put in at Eniwetok to replenish our supplies. Ten days later we left for Guam again.

"On the way to Guam we heard on the radio about the landing at Normandy. We were pleased it was a success, but we were also kind of put out because we thought we had put together the biggest amphibious landing operation ever assembled, and now we were gonna get kicked off the front page! We were glad Normandy happened, but it happened at the wrong time for us because we were real proud of what was going on in the Pacific."

"What do you remember about the Guam landing?"

"We put the first wave on the beach at 0830 on July 21, 1944. I remember when we were heading for our line of departure, we moved across the bow of a battleship, I think it was the USS *Washington*, and it fired all its 16-inch guns toward Guam at the same time. It scared the devil out of everybody. Those things were *loud* and they were only a couple hundred yards behind us. The shells went right over our heads. We hoped their gunners were accurate.

"The Japanese put up a tough defense at Guam. They had several gun emplacements on the Orote Peninsula, north of where we were landing, and they had us in their bead. An SC, a 110-foot wooden sub chaser, was engaged in operations much closer to the beach than us, well in range of the Japanese mortars. The Japanese were very skillful with their mortars. If they fired twice and didn't hit you, you'd better move before the third shell hit, because it was gonna get you. One of them hit the SC right at the 40mm gun on its bow, went on in and blew the whole bow off it. It sank. We were a couple hundred yards away, and we moved up to rescue four survivors. Other boats picked up some too. We got out of mortar range as fast as we could.

"The Japanese gun emplacements were hard to hit by naval gunfire. Navy dive-bombers flew in to give us a hand with them, and we could hear the pilots talking back and forth over the radios. One pilot did a run on a gun emplacement, and all kinds of smoke went up when he hit it. And as he flew away he said, 'Set 'em up in another alley.' Apparently they were having a good time.

"As we stayed at our post at the line of departure the landing craft came up, circled us, and lined up and then went on in. We were up 55 hours with no sleep. When things had settled down, we alternated four and four (four hours asleep, four hours on duty), and I was able to go down below. I sat down on the deck in the forward crew quarters talking to a friend of mine, and that's the last I remember. I fell asleep sitting right there.

"After all the equipment and supplies had been landed, we went ashore. I do remember one thing about Saipan and Guam both, particularly Saipan: they were just beautiful, emerald green islands. I spent quite a bit of time on Saipan; we were there while they built the air base. We saw the first B-29s land there. First time I'd seen one, and it was the biggest aircraft I'd ever seen in my life. Several of them landed at the same time. I was entranced by them.

"My ship got the responsibility of pulling aircrews out of the water if they had to ditch the aircraft on the way back to Saipan after a bombing run. We called this the dumbo run. I know that doesn't sound very nice, but we called it that because if they ended up in the water and we had to go get them, they were dumbos for being there. So we kidded them and called it the dumbo run, and they thought it was funny too. We also escorted submarines out on their runs until the water was deep enough for them to submerge.

"We did these kinds of things for a long time. We found it boring work and didn't like it. One thing that still irritates us is that we weren't involved in Iwo Jima. The ones who went there were the ones we'd operated with for so long. Some of the PCs we'd been with got to take part. We were on the dumbo run, so we didn't get to go. But we were part of the Okinawa invasion."

"What was Okinawa like?" I asked.

"Okinawa gave us a shock; it was our first introduction to the kamikazes. A bunch of our ships, mostly destroyers, had set up a radar picket line around the north part of the island. Their primary duty was to let the rest of the fleet know when Japanese aircraft headed their way.

"These destroyers had to stay out there for long periods of time, and our job was to take the mail to them. You'd think that was not very hazardous duty, but in this case it was. One day as we were passing mail over to a destroyer, a large group of kamikazes attacked it and several other ships nearby. When we heard the kamikazes were coming, we scrambled to get our lines off the destroyer. We pulled away and hauled ass, heading east. Minutes later we watched the planes coming in. The amazing thing to me was, our ships could fire everything in the world at them and they wouldn't even move. It didn't affect them at all.

"I watched one of the kamikazes slam into the port side of one destroyer. It exploded amidships and sank. I believe the planes hit and damaged several other ships in the area that day."

"What did you think when you saw these suicide attacks?"

"We had no idea what was happening, really. We'd never seen it before. That was our first experience with any kind of terrorist operation. We were amazed that anybody would do that.

"The Japanese also used a lot of suicide boats in Buckner Bay, so when we anchored there somebody had to be on watch all the time to make sure nobody came close.

"Then a typhoon blew up and forced us to leave the bay. It ran right over us. And during the typhoon, the Japanese pulled a high-altitude bombing raid on us. The problem was not that they were accurate, because Japanese bombers couldn't hit anything. But we all had to go to general quarters in the middle of that 160-mph wind."

"That must have caused you some problems," I observed.

"It did for a small vessel like us, because our bow would go under and a solid wave would go clear over our mast. That was not pleasant. Every time the bow went into the water the ship quivered. At general quarters you have a lot of people up on deck; all the guns are fully manned. All these people were totally exposed to the storm."

"Did you lose anybody overboard?"

"Fortunately, no. But it was a scary ride. We took some pretty critical rolls, maybe 50 degrees. We could see the other ships, all spread out around us, every time we hit the crest of a wave. The typhoon tossed us around like that for more than 24 hours. Many men got seasick."

"How often did you face kamikazes during the Okinawa battle?" I asked.

"They came every day for several days. We got very little sleep during that time. Even when we were off duty, we were afraid to sleep."

"Were you constantly worried one of those would hit your ship?"

"Terrified."

"So it was pretty effective as a terror tactic?"

"Absolutely."

"Did you ever go on Okinawa?"

"Briefly, to pick up a Nisei sailor who spoke Japanese. Our ship had a big set of speakers on it. We went up close to the cliffs on the north end of the island, and the Nisei tried to talk the Okinawans out of jumping."

I didn't think I'd heard him right. "Out of jumping?" I echoed.

"That's right. Civilians were jumping off the cliffs. I guess they were afraid of Americans. We moved back and forth under the cliffs, with this Japanese-American man shouting into the speakers, pleading at them not to jump. Large numbers of people jumped, including women carrying their babies, older children, old men. We were close enough to see their facial features. I personally watched dozens of them jump and land in the rocks and water at the bottom of the cliffs."

"How high were these cliffs?" I asked in disbelief.

"Quite high, possibly even a couple hundred feet high. I was stunned. I couldn't understand why they were doing this. The Nisei pleaded with them, 'Don't do it! You have nothing to fear from Americans! We will provide you with medical treatment. Please return to your villages!'"

"Had they been lied to by their leaders about how they would be treated by Americans?" I suggested, groping for an explanation.

"Possibly," he said, and the conversation faltered for a moment.

"After Okinawa," he then continued, "we went to maneuvers at Subic Bay in the Philippines to prepare for Operation Coronet. That's what the invasion of mainland Japan was to be called. We were supposed to hit one of the islands in Japan. We practiced landings for several weeks. We knew it wasn't going to be a cakewalk.

"We were tied up at Leyte and had a movie showing on the bow. It was *Madame Curie* with Greer Garson and Walter Pidgeon, and it was about the discovery of radium. This was around the 10th of August. We heard on the radio that the Japanese were considering surrendering. The atomic bombs had been dropped, but we hadn't heard about them at this point.

"We stopped the movie. This was the best news we'd heard for a long time. But a problem with the Japanese surrender had to be worked out. We didn't know what was going on other than a lot of talking back and forth between Japan and the Allies. It turned out the Japanese were trying to preserve the integrity of the emperor.

"Looking back on it now, I don't think that was the proper thing to do. I think the emperor should have been tried along with all the other war criminals. But, letting them have their way on that one point brought the war to an end.

"I think it was the 15th of August when we heard on Armed Forces Radio that Truman had announced the war was over. Everybody celebrated by hollering as much as we were allowed to while we were on duty. We had no formal celebration. We had to attend to business because we were still going to Japan, as occupiers rather than attackers now.

"The first place we landed troops was a beach near Wakayama on Honshu. We conducted the landings just as if it was a combat operation. As we escorted our transports to Japan, we reached the mouth of a channel that led into Honshu and found it had been mined.

"Our boat followed two minesweepers into shore to pick up a chart of the channel so the transports could get in. A surly Japanese naval officer came aboard and brought the charts to us. An American paratrooper officer accompanied him and translated for us. The Japanese officer went back to shore, and we took the charts out to the transports that had been waiting out there for an hour or so.

"We hadn't had any ice cream for a year. Our skipper had us signal to the lead transport, 'We have charts for you if you have ice cream for us!'" He laughed. "I don't think they'd ever had anybody deliver an ultimatum to them like that. They sent us some ice cream, so we gave them the charts.

"We put some troops on the beach near the big naval base at Kure. Some of us went ashore, and five of us went into Hiroshima."

"What did you see?"

"Devastation." He paused for a long time, trying to find words to describe the scene of an atomic bombing.

"No buildings still stood downtown, just a few on the edges of the city. A lot of the wreckage still smoldered, six weeks after the bomb had been dropped. We saw no people anywhere. The place was deserted. Cleanup hadn't even started yet."

"What did it feel like, being there?"

"I was anxious to get out, to tell the truth. The place was eerie to me. I wasn't sorry the bomb had been dropped, by any means. It just felt creepy, so still and eerie, like being on the moon. I knew one bomb had done this. We stayed about thirty minutes, and all of us decided almost at the same moment that we wanted to get out of there.

"I had just enough points to go back home almost immediately. I was one of the first men on my ship to come home. We boarded the USS *Santa Fe*, a light cruiser, at Saipan and went back on the Magic Carpet run, directly to San Francisco without even stopping at Pearl Harbor. The ship was so full a lot of men had to sleep on the deck. After serving on a little PC, the amazing thing to me about this ship was that you could walk down a deck and not get wet."

"What was the homecoming like?"

"Words are not available to describe it. We saw big signs on the hills around the bay, 'Welcome home' and things like that. The *Santa Fe* had not been back since it left the States, and it had its homecoming pennant flying from the mast. The length of the pennant is determined by the number of months overseas. That thing extended all the way from the mast to the stern.

"We tied up at the dock, welcomed by a band and a huge crowd of family members waiting for their boys. My family wasn't there; they didn't get word I was coming back. We went to Terminal Island, and they paid us for the previous four or five months. But they didn't have enough room for us to stay the night on base, so they gave a group of us a 48-hour pass. We stayed in the Mark Hopkins Hotel. In the restaurant the next morning each one of us ordered a quart of milk and a dozen eggs. We hadn't had any eggs the whole time we were overseas, except when we were about to go into combat.

"The San Francisco train depot was a madhouse. It seemed like everybody in the world was traveling at once. I looked for the window to buy a ticket to El Paso; must have been a hundred civilians in that line. The ticket agent spotted my Navy uniform and said, 'Come on up here.' So I went ahead of everybody. Got my ticket, got on the train, and went home.

"I'd told my family when I'd be home, and they were there to meet me. But they didn't recognize me when I got off the train."

He laughed. "I was five-foot-seven and 120 pounds when I left. When I came back three and a half years later, I was six-foot-one and 160. I'd been out in the sun so long in the South Pacific, my skin was the color of mahogany. They looked right past me until I got right in front of them."

William White today.

Charles Eck
Lewisville

"**I** joined the military on July 2, 1940," Charles Eck told me. "They swore us in that morning and said, 'Stand by, we're gonna put you on a train.' They were waiting for a big enough group to get together so they could send us all down to San Antonio.

"I took their instructions literally. I sat there in the recruiting station all day until four or five o'clock, and this guy came around and asked, 'What are you sittin' here for?' and I said, 'I'm waiting for you to send me wherever you're going to send me for basic training.'

"He said, 'I'm sorry, there won't be a train today. You'll have to come back.' This was on a Thursday. He said, 'There aren't any trains on Friday, Saturday, or Sunday, so come back Monday.'

"So I went back home. My mother looked at me when I showed up and said, 'What are you doing here? I thought you were going in the service.' I said, 'I *am* in the service. I got a three-day pass!' She scowled and said, 'You what?' So, I spent my second, third, and fourth days in the military on a three-day pass! And I had a ball."

"Why did you decide to join?" I asked.

Charles Eck sent this photo to his parents during the war,
signing it, "To the best parents in the world, Chuck."

"I'd completed two years of college and didn't want to go back to school, so I decided to volunteer. When I told my parents I wanted to go into the service, my dad said, 'What in the world do you want to do that for?' I said, 'Sooner or later they're gonna get me on the draft, and that means I'm gonna be a foot soldier, and I'm not interested.' I wanted to join the air corps and be an aircraft mechanic. So I joined up.

"But I got sidetracked from becoming a mechanic. I spent two weeks on the flightline at Brooks Air Force Base in San Antonio, but all I did was wash airplanes. After two weeks they called me into the office and asked, 'What would you like to do, do you want to be a mechanic?' I thought about all that airplane washing and said, 'I've had enough of that mechanic stuff.'

"I told them I'd like to learn photography and be an aerial photographer. They assigned me to guard duty while I waited for that assignment to come through. But it never came through, and instead I ended up working in the provost marshal's office.

"The major in charge of us, Roy Paige, was a good friend of a colonel in intelligence, so sometimes we helped out with a little intelligence work. One bitter cold night in February 1942 we drove down south of San Antonio, six men in two jeeps and a sedan, all equipped with two-way radios that could communicate with planes overhead and with each other. The Army had learned that airplanes were sneaking in from Mexico, flying around in the dark, and landing in south Texas somewhere, and they figured the most likely place was an open area down south of Encinal.

The major got in touch with the state highway patrol, and two patrol cars joined us.

"We drove out into the countryside and parked in the darkness. The first four nights we did this, nothing happened. But the fifth time we were in radio contact with an observer plane out of Brooks, and they flew around up there and spotted a plane approaching around 9 or 10 o'clock that night. They alerted us and we moved into position.

"A small single-engine plane, similar to a Piper Cub, came in and landed right on the open prairie. It rolled up toward us, and its landing lights shone on one of our jeeps. As soon as they saw that, the pilot started swinging that plane around so they could take off and get out of there.

"I heard over the radio, '*Stop the airplane!*' So my jeep went after it. A fella named Melvin Gambrell from Palestine, Texas, drove it, and I rode in the passenger seat with a Thompson submachine gun. We rushed out after them, and my driver circled around in front to try to get in their way. The plane pivoted away and went right back outbound, gathering speed for takeoff. But Gambrell could really wheel that jeep. We kept after them, got down to the end of the field in front of them, and the pilot turned around again to take off. This happened several times; we'd run alongside the plane and get in front of it and slow down so the pilot risked colliding with us if he kept going. We figured that would persuade the pilot to stop, but it didn't. Each time we blocked him he'd just flip the plane around. Kept going this way, that way. I kept saying to Melvin, 'Don't get too damn close!' because that propeller was right next to us."

"That must have been exciting," I said.

"I don't know if I was more excited or scared. I heard Major Paige shouting '*Stop that damn airplane!*' over the radio. Melvin said, 'Why don't you just shoot the damn tires out?'

"So I took the Thompson submachine gun and told Melvin to get me close, but not *too* close. We cut around, the pilot briefly stopped, we pulled up in front of him, and I shot a tire out. Fired a burst of two or three bullets from 10 feet away. The pilot kept going, so I fired another burst, knocking the other tire out.

"Of course then he couldn't get enough speed up to get off the ground, and the other jeep came up and helped to box them in. We had all our headlights on the plane. Then the major said over the radio, '*Shut their engine down*.'

"About that time a highway patrol car drove up, and the officer had a loudspeaker system on his car. He bellowed 'Cut the engines!' and they did.

"We closed in on the airplane. The officer said on the loudspeaker, 'One of you get out, stay in the headlights of the jeeps, and walk forward to the front of the airplane!' The pilot, who appeared to be Mexican, stepped out front and stood there. The other man followed, and we held them at gunpoint and searched them for weapons. The second man was stocky, around five foot nine, dark hair. I looked at him and did a double take. I *knew* this guy!"

He paused, pulling at his memory. "Now, let's go back several years to when I was thirteen or fourteen. My mother was born in Germany, you see, and my sister, Ruth, who was eight or nine years older than me, was interning in a hospital in Chicago where we lived. While she was working there she met a gentleman who happened to work in the

German consulate office in Chicago. She invited him over to the house to talk with my mother, because my mother didn't get much opportunity to speak German. We all got to talking to him. He spoke English very well, was very friendly, joked around.

"I told the major, 'I recognize this guy!' and explained the whole story. He ordered me to go with him in the squad car to the colonel's office at Fort Sam Houston and explain everything to him.

"The colonel's office was on the quadrangle, and he was waiting for us when we got there. I told him how I knew the man, and I told him his real name. I've been sitting here trying to remember his name and I can't except that his first name was Kurt. You'll have to forgive me; this was sixty years ago.

"The colonel told me, 'You step over here and stay in the background and listen. Don't say anything, just listen.' His men started interrogating the German, who gave some name that didn't jibe with what I knew. So one of them said, 'Kurt!' and he jerked his head up, and then they started in on him. 'You worked at the German consulate in Chicago in 1934 or 1935.' He looked startled and asked, 'How did you know that?' They didn't tell him anything and never did identify me. He spilled all the beans, told them he was coming over to make contact with somebody in Chicago who would hide him, and from there he would collect information from different German groups around Chicago.

"They took him away. I learned later the information I furnished helped to break the whole thing open, a ring of spies operating around Chicago.

"One other time, we had another mission out of the same office, a training aircraft from Brooks Field was doing some night flying and noticed somebody out east of San Antonio was flashing Morse code at it with a powerful flashlight. The base got curious about that, so we went out there at night and camped out on the prairie in pup tents. Got a bunch of ticks. We sat out there in the boonies two or three nights waiting for an airplane to pass over. And a plane finally went over and somebody started flashing lights up at it. So we immediately encircled the house. The police arrested the people there and took them off for questioning.

"I went home on leave as the war was winding down, and my dad offered me a job working for him, just like I did before the war. I had been a greaser in his garage, in other words I greased the automobiles and changed the oil. I'd also have to run and get parts for the mechanics.

"I asked my dad what it would pay this time, and he said, 'The same thing I paid you before the war,' which was $12 a week. I said, 'Hell, Dad, I make more than that now in the service! I've pulled enough grease monkey jobs for you!'

"So I stayed in the service. I later ended up in Houston working as the provost sergeant, an investigator in the provost marshal's office. That's how I met my wife. I worked with a lieutenant, a good friend of mine, who went all the way back to World War I. His name was Canaan, but we always called him Pop. He was in charge of investigations.

"Somebody stole a whole bunch of parachutes and flak jackets. Pop got a tip about a lieutenant who was flashing around and trying to sell scarves that had been made by cutting a parachute apart. We took this man in for questioning. We used the friend and foe method, you know, good guy, bad guy. Pop told me to talk rough to him. So I did. I told him, 'You're a pitiful S-O-B for an officer.' I cut it loose real bad, told him what a lowdown creature he was, called him all kinds of profanities, everything under the sun."

I looked at this tall, thin, soft-spoken man and tried to imagine a torrent of swear words coming out of his mouth. I just couldn't picture it.

"Funny thing was, there was a lady in there, a real good steno clerk, taking everything down verbatim in shorthand. A young, pretty gal named Patricia Higgins. I'd been trying to date her for quite some time. And here she was, listening to all this foul language!

"The lieutenant finally got scared and spilled the beans, so we went out to his house. We put him in the backseat of the car, and Pop sat with him while I drove. We went into his house and filled up the whole trunk of this four-door sedan with stolen materiel, loaded up the passenger seat in front, and then piled more on the floor in back. Pop and this guy were sitting there in the backseat covered up to the neck with stolen supplies. We drove back and unloaded it all.

"But the bad part was, I tried to get a date again with the steno clerk, and she really let me have it. She said, 'I wouldn't go out with you for anything. The way you chewed out that officer was pitiful!' I was only a tech sergeant at the time, see.

"She wouldn't speak a word to me after that. Pop finally took her over to one side and explained the situation, and

Charles Eck with Patricia Higgins,
the woman he married.

then she came over and apologized for speaking to me that way.

"I said, 'Do I get a date or no?' And she said, 'Yeah, I'll give you a date.'

"Four months later Patricia and I got married."

Charles Eck today.

Lord, just get me out of this
and I promise I won't come back

Gisela Botzenmayer
Stan Prather
Arlington

Gisela Botzenmayer, a cheery and energetic German lady, knows hospitality. She had prepared a generous tray of strawberries, grapes, cheese, and crackers for my visit, and she offered me a glass of wine. We relaxed and chatted at length and then I turned on the tape recorder. Stan Prather sat in an easy chair nearby and listened. Occasionally, Gisela threw in a German word, and I'd stop her and ask what it meant—and how to spell it.

"I was born in 1928 in Sondershausen, in the state of Thüringen, which they call the green heart of Germany," she said in a crisp accent. "Germany went to war in 1938, but for us in Sondershausen life was beautiful. I had a good childhood with no worries. My brother, Karlheinz, and I lived in a nice house, a nanny took care of us, and we had plenty to eat. My father, Karl Botzenmayer, taught at the school. Then the war broke out and the army drafted him. He spoke French and English, so he became an interpreter for Rommel."

Gisela Botzenmayer at age 6, on her first
day of school. She is holding a *zuckertute*,
a traditional package of goodies including
school supplies and candy.

"You're kidding," I said. This meant I could now play six degrees of separation with Field Marshal Erwin Rommel, the best-known German general from World War II.

She showed me a photograph of a tall, handsome man next to Rommel, both standing tall in their German army uniforms. In front of them stood two men, one a pudgy officer with a round hat. "That's my dad with Rommel, and I think these men are French and British officers who had just surrendered. The Germans took thousands of Allied prisoners of war that day, French, English, Scottish, at St. Valery-en-Caux. These people were from the 51st Highland Division and the 10th French Army.

This photo shows Field Marshal Erwin Rommel, at left, accepting the surrender at St. Valery-en-Caux of a French officer (foreground). Karl Botzenmayer, in center of photo, interprets for Rommel.

Gisela Botzenmayer's father, Karl, was drafted into the German army and served as an interpreter.

"When Rommel went to Africa, my father couldn't go along because he had stomach ulcers, and the doctor said the dust from the desert wouldn't be good for him. He was released from the army. In the meantime a lot of German people were relocating to Poland, which Germany had captured in 1939. They opened schools for the German dependents who came over to be with the soldiers. My father went to teach in one of those German schools at Lodz. So we lived with him in Wartegau, the region around Lodz, from 1942 to 1945.

"In January of 1945 the war was raging in *Altdeutschland*, the old Germany before the war. Stan and my now-deceased husband were dropping their bombs there. Meanwhile those of us in Poland were getting bombed by the Russians, and the Red Army was heading our way.

"The *Volkssturm*—civil defense—took Karlheinz at the age of fifteen, and a lot of other boys his age. They gave him a *panzerfaust*, the German equivalent of a bazooka, and they had the boys dig ditches. They told him and another little kid to get into one ditch. These kids were so tiny, my brother was a shrimp at that age, it took two of them to hold the weapon. The first boy put it on his shoulder and the second one fired it. The Volkssturm told these kids, 'Wait until the enemy tank rolls right over you and then fire into its belly.'

She looked at me intently. "You know what that would do to the kids in the ditch, right?"

"Right," I said grimly.

"So my brother and a bunch of other kids deserted and went home. The military would have shot them if they got caught. Then on the 17th of January the Volkssturm went out with loudspeakers all over Lodz and told all the Germans we had to leave, but not to worry, just take what we can carry and we'd be back soon. Well, we weren't going to be back soon because the Russians were coming.

Gisela Botzenmayer at age 16.

"And that was the start of the Big Trek, where hundreds of thousands of people tried to get away from the Russians and escape to Altdeutsch. My family left our home with a sled and what we could carry. My mother, Hilda, wore her hair like Betty Grable. She hid her jewels on top of her head and combed her hair over the whole shebang. We loaded up our sled with what we could but had to leave so much behind. We had a nice house but couldn't take any of the beautiful furniture with us.

"Even though my father was a civilian now, the Volkssturm took him like they did all German men toward the end of the war. They all got drafted, even the old ones. They pulled in everybody they could find; I swear to God our neighbor had one leg and they pulled him in. These men were supposed to defend the home front. My father had the job of digging trenches.

"So it was just me, my mother, and my brother making the trek. We started off in the middle of the night with no clue where my father was. But we had agreed that if it came to the point where we had to leave without him, we would either go to the Munich area where my father was from, or we would go to my mother's family in Zorbig, a town near Halle.

"So we started to follow the thousands of people walking in the direction of Germany. Walking back through Poland wasn't easy because many of the Polish weren't too friendly to us Germans, of course. A few were sympathetic but some were downright nasty."

"You had to pull the sled by hand?" I asked.

"Yes, and it was the middle of January, and Poland is right next to Russia, so the snow was like this." She held her hand at neck level. "Needless to say, nobody had cars. Some people had horses and carriages but 90 percent of us had to walk. As we walked we started to see people's belongings left in piles on the side of the road. After miles and miles of walking, people couldn't carry so many belongings anymore so they just let them go.

"German soldiers returning from the Eastern Front passed us in slowly moving trains, carrying their wounded. They spotted my mother's Red Cross uniform, and they pulled her and me into the boxcar because they needed some nurses. But they didn't want my brother. They said, 'The boy can walk,' but my mother said, 'No, I'm not going anywhere unless I can take my children.'

"We were lucky, we rode a while, then walked again, then rode a while. The most horrible thing I remember is this big flatbed truck passed by, and a group of us walking along the road asked if we could sit in the back. They said, 'Yeah, get on.'

"So many people climbed on we had to stand. A lumpy tarpaulin covered the truck bed, and we were standing on it. One of the people pulled the corner of the tarpaulin back to see what was under there that was so hard to stand on. And it was all dead German soldiers, lined up like sardines."

"How did you react?" I asked.

"I threw up."

"You'd been standing right on top of them?"

"Right on them. They were frozen stiff.

"I remember another thing—some things I remember from my mother telling me, because you can block the really bad things out. Sometimes I remember something very vividly and my brother, who was right there, remembers something totally different, and he remembers some things where I have a total mental block.

"A whole bunch of us clustered together for safety in numbers in an abandoned Polish barn for the night. My mother had brought an alarm clock. She set it every night so we wouldn't linger too long in any one place. We knew we had to get away before the Russians reached us.

"A group we called the White Russians were more sympathetic to us than the other Russians, and when they came across us they would tell us, 'Hey, you better get a move on, because they're right on your heels.' One night we slept in a barn with a lot of other people, and the alarm clock went off of its own accord at three in the morning. Mom, being a little bit superstitious, said 'That's an omen. We must leave at once.' So a group of us started walking again. But many of the people didn't want to get up yet and stayed.

"The next day we heard from other people who caught up with us that in the middle of the night the Russians came and rolled through the barn with their tanks, right over all those people.

"When we finally reached old Germany, we got to experience the American and British bombing. Very heavy bombing. This is where Stan comes in, because he dropped bombs in exactly the same area where I was at this time: Liepzig, Halle, Magdeburg.

"We stayed at my maternal grandparents' house in Zorbig. We still had no clue where my father was. We endured a lot of bombing then, a *lot* of bombing. This was toward the end of the war. The propaganda from Goebbels was unbelievable. We thought we were still winning the war! Meanwhile the bombing got heavier and heavier. We heard the bombers a long time before we saw them. A deep humming noise. And they dropped what we called the *Weinachtsbaum*, the Christmas Tree."

"She's talking about the Royal Air Force bombing at night and dropping Pathfinder flares from the lead plane to mark the target," Stan offered.

"Then the Americans would do the *teppig bomben*, carpet-bombing, just one explosion after another in a row. An air raid warden watched over us, and we got punished if we didn't do what we were supposed to do. We had to keep our windows dark. We laid our clothes out at night so at a moment's notice we could jump into them and hurry down to the basement.

"There was also a steel-reinforced air raid shelter we could go to. We did that for a while, but it became exhausting and we finally decided whatever happens, happens.

"One day we heard a roar, looked out the window, and saw American tanks rolling into town. The Americans occupied lots of homes and kicked the residents out, including my grandfather's house where we were staying. We got lucky because my grandparents were good friends with the postman, and he let us sleep in the post office in the room where they stored the packages. I remember one funny thing, my grandfather always had a vegetable garden, and after the Americans started living in our house, we actually snuck through the picket fence into our own garden to steal some of our own vegetables!"

We laughed.

"The Americans were very good; I can't remember anything negative about them. By that time we had gotten word my father was alive and in Munich. Remember how after September 11 people in New York posted notes in public asking for information about missing people? We located my father the same way.

"Then one day we looked out the window, and we couldn't believe it; over there at the courthouse where there had been an American flag, now there was a hammer and sickle."

"Uh-oh," I said.

"That's right, a Soviet flag. Our town was in the territory that the Allies handed to the Russians on a silver platter. That's when all heck broke loose. The Russians weren't like the Americans, who were all nice and clean; they looked like animals. They came on little horses and bicycles, and they were extremely dirty. Right away they raped an eighty-year-old lady next door.

"After a couple of weeks, my grandfather said, 'We've got to get the women out of here.' We were all young women; I was sixteen, my mother was thirty-six, my aunts were twenty-three and thirty-four. One day we heard a knock at the door. My grandfather answered the door, and the Russians said, 'Where are all the young girls we've seen around here?'

"My grandfather had the presence of mind to say, 'Oh, they don't live with us, they were just here for a visit. They're not here any more.' I'll never forget that night. In our laundry room we had one of those big vats where we soaked our clothes in cold water all night to bleach them up before we boiled them clean. When it wasn't in use the kettle was empty, so that night he put us all in there. It was big enough to hold us and put the lid on top of us. He said, 'They will be back. You have to get out of here.'

"We got out, my mother, my brother, one of my aunts, and myself. My mother used the jewelry she had salvaged, and I'm not talking about the crown jewels but ordinary jewelry, to pay an ex-soldier to lead us out. He knew the territory very well.

"Germany had been divided into the British, French, Russian, and American sectors now, and we had to get through all the others to get to the American zone. We knew the Americans were the most humane. We traveled only at night, crossed over no man's land, and ended up in a suburb of Munich and reunited with my father.

"Of course all the schools were closed. Nothing was open. My father found work at an air base the Americans had taken over, teaching French to the Americans. The job didn't pay money, it paid in food. In order to get a rationing card in Germany you had to have a job.

"Father wanted to get me into an office job, but they wouldn't take me because I had gone to an all-girls school. In Germany the school system is different. If you want to learn how to type, you go to a trade school. So I had never learned. But they let me work as a waitress in the officers' mess hall, which was a very good thing. By German standards it was a degrading job, but it was good because I was close to the food. So when the mess sergeant made doughnuts and threw the extra dough away, I would bring it home and we would have doughnuts.

"I started working there in October 1945. After three or four months I noticed this one officer always sat at one of my two tables, come heck or high water. I had learned to speak just a little English, so the officers got a big kick out of sitting at my table and listening to my horrible English. If my tables were full but other tables were available, this one officer named John Stearns would go to the pool table and play snooker until a seat became available at my table. What can I say? I was young, and he was young and gorgeous and kind, and to make a long story short, we fell in love."

"What did your parents think about this?" I asked.

"They weren't too thrilled, and his parents were horrified. John was from Barry, Illinois, which, I don't think there's even 1,000 people, there might be 300 counting the chickens. When he told his parents he wanted to marry a German girl, oh my God, how could he? I think the planet Mars would have been better than coming from Germany. In their minds, anyone from Germany was a Nazi.

"Then John had to ask my father for my hand, and that was a terrible thing because in my parents' generation, the parents picked who you should marry, and here I was, their only daughter, marrying a stranger and going off. And I wasn't even eighteen yet.

"But they liked John and eventually gave their approval. So John told his commanding officer, and he didn't like the idea either. At the time lots of enlisted men wanted to marry German girls but not so many officers. His superiors told him, 'You're supposed to set an example. You just don't know our gorgeous American girls, our long-stemmed roses. You're just desperate.'

"So they sent him back to the States, hoping the romance would fizzle out. They sent him to Florida for four months, to air inspector's school. He told me we would get married one way or another, even if he had to give up his citizenship.

"Well, after about forty years of marriage, I used to ask him all the time, 'Would you still give up your citizenship to marry me?' And he would say, 'Oh, I don't know...'

"I still have the letter he wrote to his parents, telling them he fell in love with this German girl, but she's not a Nazi! And he underlined that point. I still have the letter his parents wrote back to him, and they said, 'If that's the girl you want, then you should marry her.' We had a beautiful formal wedding in a chateau the Americans had taken over and turned into an officer's club. John asked his commanding officer if he could have the chateau for one day for the reception, and his commander said yes. In the German black market you could get a lot with cigarettes, so John took twelve cartons of cigarettes and traded them to get everything we needed for the wedding. My wedding gown was made out of a parachute. It had a 12-foot train. John's commander, Col. Woodbury, served as best man. John and I were married fifty-one years."

She asked me, "Do you know how we met, Stan and I?"

"No," I said.

"He lost a wife to cancer, and I lost a husband to cancer. Our spouses were at the same time getting chemotherapy at Arlington Cancer Center. One day at the hospital John wore his World War II jacket. He had been a P-51 pilot during the war. His jacket said 'P-51' and 'Bluenosed Bastards of Bodney,' that was the 352nd Fighter Group, a very famous outfit. A nurse told him, 'There's a man in the booth right next to you whose wife has cancer, and I think he was in

The wedding of John Stearns and Gisela Botzenmayer.
Gisela's wedding dress is made out of a parachute.

World War II. I think you should meet him.' And that's how
Stan and John met."

Stan took up the story.

"The nurse introduced me to John, and we chatted for a while and then I returned to my wife, Doris. Later I went up to the desk to arrange her next chemo appointment. John stood there in front of me, making an appointment for himself. I heard him say something about 'November 2nd, 1944,' and without even thinking about it, it just clicked in my memory and I said 'Merseburg, Germany!'

"He turned around and said, 'What did you say?'

"I repeated myself and he said, 'How'd you know about that?'

"I said, 'I was there.'

"It turned out his fighter group escorted my bomber group over the target on that day. I told him, 'If you'd pointed your nose at us, I'd probably have confused the P-51 with an ME-109 and taken a shot at ya.' That's how he and I met."

"So the four of us always had lunch together after that," Gisela said. "I lost my husband, and nine months later Stan lost his wife. She's been gone now three years. But we're still alive and enjoying life, and we're thankful for what we've got."

"That's quite a story," I said, and then I turned to Stan. "Let's hear about *your* experiences during the war."

"Oh, I don't have anything interesting to tell," he said coyly.

"Sure you don't," I said with a grin. "Let's start with where you were on December 7, 1941."

He nodded and thought for a moment. "Sunday morning. I was playing football on the quadrangle at the entrance to Fort Sam Houston in San Antonio. I lived near there. The quadrangle was outside the entrance to the base,

The young Stan Prather.

and my friends and I used to go over and play sandlot football all the time. We'd all graduated from high school in June of 1940. Those of us whose daddies could afford it went to college, but I was in the other half. There was no *way* I'd get to go to college.

"We played till 10 or 11 o'clock in the morning until we were tired and walked across the street to a drugstore to buy some pops. I remember vividly the sign above the door that said, 'No dogs or enlisted men allowed.' That's how people looked upon the military in pre-war times. That attitude was about to change in a hurry.

"We got some cold drinks and heard the radio. They were talking about an attack on Pearl Harbor. We listened for a while and then walked back to finish our game. I remember hearing somebody say, 'Who or what in the world is Pearl Harbor?' We had no idea. And that was my introduction into World War II. After the game we just went home, did our thing. It didn't really dawn on us that we were in a war, and if we were in a war, well how about that? We had no idea what it meant.

"The only job I'd been able to get up until that point was working at a filling station, pumping gas or whatever needed to be done, working fourteen to sixteen hours a day for a dollar a day. But I couldn't work all seven days of the week because the owner couldn't afford to pay me every day. I'd work when he had an extra dollar.

"When Pearl Harbor happened and things started picking up, I was able to get a better job out at Duncan Field as a clerk in the receiving department of the air materiel command there. I made $105 a month. My mother was a widow, and she and I rented a five-room house for $25 a month.

"My uncle ran a café on Broadway Street, and my mom worked as a waitress there. I never was called up for the draft. I worked at Duncan Field until September 1942. Then one day I was riding home on the bus with a man I worked with, an old, old guy."

"How old?"

"Thirty-four." We laughed. "We got off the bus in downtown San Antonio to make a transfer and walked across Houston Street. There happened to be an Army recruiter's office there.

"I'd always wanted to fly, but the Army Air Force had required a minimum of two years college before you could even apply. And I never gave any thought to entering any other branch.

"But then the military waived the two years of college rule. High school graduates who could pass a written test could now apply. I made an off-hand comment as we walked by the recruiter's office, 'One of these days I'm gonna go up there and take that test, see if I can pass it.'

"The man I was with said, 'Well, let's both go take it right now.' So we went up to the second floor and took it. A blind man could have passed that test. Nothing to it." He chuckled.

"We both passed it, and they told us, 'If you can pass the physical exam tomorrow morning at Fort Sam Houston, you can get into the cadet program.' What I didn't know was, this thirty-four-year-old was a con man of the first order. I had recently bought a 1937 Plymouth, and he didn't have a car. He'd been in an automobile accident many years before and ruined his knee. No way could he pass that physical. He knew it, and I never gave it a thought.

"I passed the physical and I was in the Army, and he bought my car from me. That was what he was after the whole time!"

We laughed.

"Officially I was an aviation cadet, but they placed me on inactive service because so many people were joining up they couldn't accept them all at once. They told me, 'Wait a few weeks, we'll call you.'

"A week passed and they didn't call so I went back and said, 'Come on, when am I going in?' I went every week and they always told me the same thing: 'Go away, we'll call you, don't bother us anymore. I don't want to see your face up here again.'

"It took six months before they took me, in March of 1943."

Stan's granddaughter, Kristin, arrived for a visit. Gisela let her in and she sat down nearby to listen.

"I got on the train at the station near the Alamo in downtown San Antonio. I was going with Doris at the time, the girl I later married. Her parents got three gallons of gas a week so she borrowed her parents' car and drove me down there. I was allowed to take one small suitcase and what I had on my back. So I got on the choo choo train, and I was in the military.

"I ended up in Santa Ana, California, for preflight training. We were in our ninth and last week of training, and they posted a sheet on the bulletin board in the barracks that said, 'Sign up here for your preference, multi-engined or single-engined.'

"Of course everybody wanted to fly peashooters. Most fighter planes were single-engined, so that's what everybody signed up for.

"I was just about to sign up the same way, just getting ready to write my name, when somebody hollered, 'Hey Tex, come over here, you got to see this!'

"I ran to the barracks door, and here comes a shiny new P-38 out of Burbank, Calif., just out of the factory, flying low and slow and showing off for all us cadets. The P-38 had two engines, so I immediately ran back and signed up for multi-engine.

"Then we got our orders to go to primary flight training. I ended up 30-odd miles outside Tempe, Arizona, at Thunderbird Field No. 2. I made it more than halfway through the program, homesick and lonesome all the time, and Doris and I decided to get married. The cadets were not supposed to get married. And I didn't tell anybody I'd done it.

"I washed out shortly thereafter. They told me, 'Obviously you can't obey orders, how can you give orders?'"

"How did they figure it out?" I asked.

"I have no idea. But, my mind certainly wasn't on flying anymore; it was on her. I went to washout court, and I was only allowed to use three phrases no matter what the question was: yes sir, no sir, no excuse sir. They asked me, 'Is there any reason why you shouldn't be washed out?' And I had no reason so I said 'No sir.' Then they asked, 'Would you like us to send your papers back to Santa Ana, to see if they'll reclassify you as a bombardier or navigator?' Absolutely I wanted that, so I said, 'Yes sir.'

"I remained in limbo there until word came up from Santa Ana that they were only accepting bombardier/navigators. You had to be willing to take dual training if you wanted to go there. But when we had first arrived at preflight and had to fill out our preferences on a scale of 1 to 10, pilot, bombardier, or navigator, I had put 1 for pilot, 2 for bombardier, and 10 for navigator. I'd never taken trigonometry in high school so I'd figured I'd never pass navigation.

"These people saw that and said, 'Obviously you don't want to be a navigator so we can't accept you.'"

Kristin and Gisela had been talking quietly at the dinner table. I noticed them looking at a photograph and giggling. Kristin came over and showed me a very recent picture of Stan, wearing his flight suit from the war.

"Wow!" I said. "It still fits. That's amazing."

Kristin and Gisela laughed.

"It's a little tight," Stan said with a satisfied smile.

Kristin showed me another picture of Stan lifting himself up into the hatch of a B-17. It's done by hanging from the hatch with your hands and lifting your legs past your head into the hatch and pulling yourself in. And this picture, too, was very recent. I was impressed.

"After that," Stan continued, "They sent me to Amarillo for reassignment. A second lieutenant there told me, 'You've got three choices. You can stay here in Amarillo and go to aircraft engine mechanic school and then aerial gunnery school. You can go to Lowry Field in Denver, Colorado, and go to armament school and then aerial gunnery school. Or, you can go to Springfield, Illinois, and go to radio operator training and then aerial gunnery school.'

Stan Prather shows he hasn't lost his touch by swinging up into a B-17 while on a trip to England in 2001.

"I said, 'I don't want to be a gunner.'

"The second lieutenant said, 'You've got three choices . . .' and went through the same list all over again.

"I said, 'No, sir, I will not volunteer. I don't want to go to gunnery school.'

"He gave me a sergeant's name and told me to report to him. Turned out it was the mess sergeant. I pulled KP and waited tables for a long time. After that the mess sergeant sent me back to the lieutenant, and he said, 'You've got three choices . . .'"

"Ah, I see how it works now," I said, laughing.

"I told him, 'I'm not going to gunnery school, sir.' He told me to report back to the mess sergeant. I went through three or four episodes of that until the last time, they had me scrubbing out garbage cans. I don't know what they would have done if I'd refused again. They probably would have shot me.

"I finally broke and said 'OK, I'll go.' I chose armament school and was transferred to Denver. It was the middle of December, cold and snowy. I'd never seen snow in my life. I graduated from armament school as a private first class.

"They sent me to Las Vegas for aerial gunnery school, and I graduated as a corporal. From there they sent me to a repple depple at Salt Lake City for reassignment. I sat around there for a couple of weeks. I managed to get into trouble, but I won't go into all that."

"Oh, come on," I urged.

"They called us all out one morning to assign us to bomber crews," he continued, ignoring me. "Every flight crew had a pilot, a copilot, a navigator, a bombardier, and six gunners. We stood on a field in the dark and the cold and the snow, and they started calling out names.

"They called out ten names and the crew number and told us to assemble under that number. They said, 'Once you've assembled with your flight crew, look around. There's ten of you there. Learn about all the other guys, because from this point forward you're gonna live, sleep, and eat with them.'

"I waited and waited and waited until I was the very last man standing there, and finally they called out my name, crew 38C. I joined my crew and started shaking hands, and they asked where I was from. I said, 'I'm your token Texan.'

"They said, 'Oh my God, we got a Texan.' Three of them came from California, two from Pennsylvania, two from New York, one from Virginia—"

"All Yankees!" Gisela cried.

"And then there was me," Stan said.

We laughed. "How did you get along with them?" I asked.

"Oh, fine. We all got along." He paused. "Well, I take that back. We didn't get along too well with the navigator. He went through our combat crew training and went overseas with us. But before we went into combat, his relationship with the enlisted men got so bad that six of us went to the pilot, M. C. Johnson. To this day he won't tell me his first name, just goes by M. C.

"The pilot was the aircraft commander, so he could do something about the navigator if he wanted to. We told him, 'We will not fly if that man remains as part of this crew.'

263

"We really had no right to say such a thing. They could tell us to do whatever they wanted to. But theoretically, you did have to volunteer to fly. Theoretically. Even in wartime. If you refused to fly into combat, that was OK; they'd throw you in the infantry, and you'd go into combat just the same."

"Wasn't that considered mutiny?"

"You could refuse to fly. But you would get reassigned, and they'd make darn sure they put you into some infantry outfit and send you into combat. You'd just signed your own death warrant, essentially.

"We don't know what happened after we spoke to Johnson, but one day our navigator disappeared and a new one joined our crew."

"Tell me more about this navigator."

"We went for combat training at Dalhart, Texas. This was supposed to be a six-week program, after which we would fly to the port of embarkation to get sent overseas. We made it through five weeks at Dalhart and they told us, 'We're going to have to transfer you somewhere else. They're bringing in a new top secret bomber, and we can't fly B-17s here any more.' The secret bomber turned out to be the B-29, but we didn't know that at the time.

"They sent us to Tampa, Florida. At Dalhart we'd been in the 2nd Air Force but now we were in the 3rd Air Force. We thought we only had one more week to go but they said, 'You'll have to start over. We don't think the 2nd Air Force trains you right. We're going to train you our way.' So we started over.

"About this time the flight engineer got married, and his wife came up to visit him. Things got so bad there at

Tampa, they all called us the Dalhart crew. We didn't get along with them at all. They had surprise roll calls and all ten men better answer up. If one guy was missing for any reason, we'd call out and answer for him. And we got away with it.

"The flight engineer went off to be with his bride and didn't get back in time, so we answered for him. We cut a little hole in the fence for him to get through to join back up with us. That went on for quite a while. When we finished the six weeks, the detachment commander said, 'Well, gentlemen, I'm sending you overseas as quick as I can. You're going straight to POE (point of embarkation) and you're gone. You're out of my hair.'

"He was supposed to give us ten days leave before sending us overseas, but he wasn't going to do it. Well, one of the guys was the son of a congressman. He called his father, who pulled some strings.

"So the detachment commander told us, 'I'm required to give you ten days leave before sending you overseas, but I am not required to give you travel time, so you've got ten days to go home and come back and that's it.'"

"Nice," I said.

"That's right, he didn't endear himself to us. We got back from all our homes ten days later, and the commander said, 'Ha! I've got you bastards now. You're on your way. Get on that train and get the hell out of here.' We thought we were gonna travel the ocean by train the way he was talking to us.

"The train took us to Langley Field in Virginia, where we spent six weeks taking radar training." He looked at his granddaughter, Kristin. "Your daddy was born while I was there."

"We went to Boeing in Seattle to pick up a brand new airplane, flew it back, and packed all our gear in it. Then they put us on overseas alert. Every morning we climbed into the airplane and waited out on the taxiway, and the tower always told us, 'Kill your engines and await further instructions.' We had to just sit there; we couldn't leave the plane for anything. At about three or four o'clock in the afternoon the tower would say, 'You won't be flying today. Report back to barracks.'

"One day I got word from San Antonio that my baby had been born. I went to the chaplain and told him my tale of woe and asked if I could get emergency leave to see my new son. This is his answer, verbatim: 'Son, you were there for the laying of the keel. You don't have to be there for the launching of the ship.'"

Kristin and Gisela hooted with laughter.

"We'd been having trouble getting our mail because we hadn't been assigned to a specific barracks; we just slept any place we could find empty bunks. And they wouldn't bring the mail out to the airplane. So one crewmember would get detail every day to sneak off the airplane, go pick up the mail, and bring it to us. This was against the rules, but we got away with it the whole time.

"This day it was the copilot's turn. He and I were about the same size. He said, 'Tex, come up here and sit in my chair so the tower can see there's two people in the cockpit.' And he went to get the mail.

"We were sitting there after he left, and all of a sudden the tower comes on, 'Tail No. 358, start your engines and prepare to taxi!'

"Now this would have been desertion in the face of the enemy if our copilot wasn't with us when we took off. It was a very serious offense for which the penalty could be severe. We were looking frantically around for Bob. 'Where the hell is he? I can't see him.' We had no way to contact him. We didn't dare to get off the airplane.

"The tower says again, '358, start your engines! Get moving!'

"So we proceeded to start the four engines as slowly as possible. The tower called again. '358, *move!*' We taxied *very* slowly toward the runway, and thank God, somebody said, 'There's a jeep tearing down the runway behind us!' And there was the copilot waving at us. We transferred him while in motion from the jeep to the waist door of the B-17, got him up in the cockpit just in time to get to the runway and tell the tower, 'We are here.'

"They said, 'No you're not, you're out of here.' As soon as we got airborne, the copilot passed out the mail."

"Wow," I said.

"Now, while we'd been at Langley I'd sprained my ankle. It was raining and I had GI shoes with rubber heels on, and I came running out onto the porch and slipped. I couldn't march but they let me fly. We flew to Goose Bay, Labrador, on the way to England, and they assigned us to a Quonset hut for the night. It had a four-inch-high step on the bottom frame of the door, and because of that bad leg I tripped on that thing, fell outside, and sprained the *other* ankle.

"They took me over to the dispensary. The doctor thought I was trying to screw off and get out of combat. He kept going on about how his son was in combat overseas, *blah blah blah*, and finally I understood what he was thinking, and I said, 'Doc, can't you just fix me up good enough to leave me on flying status? I don't want to go back to the States.'

"He said, 'Oh, you don't want to go back?' All of a sudden I was a hero. He gave me a pair of crutches and said, 'Use these, and I'll clear you to fly.' And I left Goose Bay, Labrador, on crutches.

"From there we flew to Reykjavik, Iceland, and then to RAF Valley in Wales. When we landed there, the other nine guys got off first, I handed my crutches out, and then I just grabbed onto the top of the door and swung out. A sergeant stood there who'd already been overseas three years. He saw me, shook his head in dismay, and said, 'Oh my God, they're even sending crippled boys over now!'

"You asked about the navigator, and that's what I've been leading up to. Before the flight from Labrador to Iceland, we'd been briefed that if we had to ditch the plane or bail out over the ocean, our life expectancy in that cold water would be no more than thirty minutes. The plane was cold too. I was back in the waist section just aft of the radio room, and we had all kinds of supplies packed in the airplane, rations and things. So I made myself a bed back there. I had a heavy sheepskin-lined jacket and pants. I was snug as a bug, sleeping away, and here comes this navigator. 'Tex, wake up, wake up!'

"'What do you want?'

"'Get out of there!'

Stan Prather's flight crew at their base at Deopham Green in England.

"'What do you mean, get out of here?'

"'Get out of here, go up in the radio room, go somewhere else.'

"'Why?'

"He says, 'Because I'm ordering you to. That's an order.'

"I stared at him and said, 'I'm not moving out of here.'

"He said, 'I'll report you to the pilot.'

"I said, 'Let's go up and talk to him right now.'

"All he wanted was my warm bed. That's the kind of guy he was. He was constantly doing that type of thing. He was absolutely convinced God made him an officer so he could have enlisted men serve his every need. That was why the six of us said, 'No way.' It wasn't just me; it was all of us. The pilot must have felt it too, because one morning suddenly we had a different navigator.

"Our original navigator was assigned to a different crew. Later after we'd started flying combat missions, we asked some of the guys on that crew how they liked their navigator. They said, 'He's not on our crew any more.'

"We asked why and they said, 'He fell out of the bomb bay.'"

"Oh, boy..."·I said.

"Yeah, right," Gisela said sardonically. "Fell out."

"They should have dropped him over Germany and let you guys have him," Stan kidded her. "We'd have won the war right there."

"What was your first combat mission like?" I asked.

"We hit Wiesbaden, Germany, on September 19, 1944. Munich was our primary target, but when we were almost there word came over that the Germans had thrown up a very effective smokescreen, so we diverted to the secondary target, a Wiesbaden tank factory. I flew as right waist gunner. You can't see much out of the waist. You can only see to the side; can't see forward because the wing's in the way and can't see back because of the tail. I could hear the guy up in front calling out 'Flak, 12 o'clock level,' and we started to see the flak bursts.

"I remember hanging on to my .50-caliber machine gun mounted on an iron post. The airplane was bouncing around because of air turbulence from the formation. A flak burst shook the plane and knocked me down to my knee, still hanging on that gun, praying very carefully to the Lord, 'You just get me out of this and I promise I won't come back.' That's how bad that mission was. Of course I broke that promise!

"Somebody said, 'Look at that B-17 at three o'clock.' That was my side. I looked out and saw the pilot of the other plane had put his landing gear down, which was the signal for 'Let me out of formation, I'm in trouble.' The planes spread out to let him through and he pulled up. I remember seeing a cloud of white smoke back there.

"No fighters hit us that day, but the flak was bad enough. The Germans didn't know our altitude because radar wasn't that good, but they knew our course, and once we committed to the bomb run they knew we had to fly at a fixed speed and altitude and could not take evasive action. So they built a three-dimensional box in the sky with flak bursts, and we just had to fly through it. It was a matter of luck for both sides. Normally they fired a four-gun pattern so we saw bursts in fours. We could actually hear the bursts if the flak got close. When it got close enough that we could see the red flash in the middle of the black puff of smoke, that was too close. Damned close."

"How many missions did you fly?" I asked.

"I'm credited with thirty-three completed."

"What were some of your worst ones?"

He opened a folder and read through some notes. While he chose a mission to talk about, Kristin told me, "Over Christmas we spent three days recording their war memories. They've got really good attention to detail, and I got twelve hours of videotape."

"Twelve hours?" I echoed. "That's fantastic. It's really great that you preserved all that material."

Stan had made his choice. "After my second mission, which was over Merseburg, we debriefed, went to chow, and returned to our barracks. We were all sitting around in

A B-17 named Four Freedoms opens its bomb bay doors.

there and someone came in from headquarters and said, 'Tex, you're to report over to the squadron commander immediately.'

"I saw three other guys waiting to see the commander too. We were all from different flight crews, and the only thing we had in common was that we were all washed-out cadets. Got to talking to them, trying to figure out why we'd been summoned. We hadn't done anything wrong that we knew about. We were taken in to see the commander, who told us, 'We lost seven bombardiers on that mission.'

"Suddenly we had little lightbulbs going on over our heads. He had our personnel files on his desk. He said, 'You four gentlemen have all been in the cadet program.'

A B-17 in formation drops its bombs.

A B-17 shows extensive damage after a
rough mission on December 24, 1944.

"'Yes . . . '

"He said, 'You've all had training on the bombsight.'

"And we said, very cautiously, 'Yeeesss . . . . '"

"He repeated, 'We lost a lot of bombardiers today,' and I remember thinking, 'Major, you were flying this desk, we were up there. *We're* the ones who lost of lot of bombardiers.'

"Anyway, it was pretty obvious he wanted us to fly in the nose as bombardiers.

"We couldn't say anything standing there at attention, but he said, 'The four of you know what I want. It's a voluntary position. You don't have to take it.' I could read between the lines, 'But you really ought to.'

"He told us, 'Go out and report back to me in one hour. Talk it over and come back and let me know your decision.'

"We went outside and talked it over. 'We lost seven today and there's only four of us! They must be out of their minds.'

"We went back. I was the tallest of the four so I was on the left when we stood in formation, and that made me the spokesman. He said, 'Gentlemen, have you reached a decision?'

"I said, 'Yes, sir, we've talked it over. We've mutually decided we'd prefer to stay with our present flight crews.'

"He said, 'Fine! I got your papers right here.'

"He got around us by changing our MOS (military occupational specialty) to enlisted bombardier. They just called us toggleers since all we did was toggle off the bombs. So, for my third mission I became a toggleer. They left me with my crew. Our bombardier was out of action because a burst of flak had hit right in front of the plane and blew glass out of the nose bubble. He had just pulled his goggles up on top of his head to put his eye down on the bombsight, and the glass went into his eyes and blinded him. Now I would get to sit in his chair.

"I flew with my original crew through my 17th mission. After that I started to accompany new crews flying on their first, second, or third mission. I'd go with them as an experienced hand to help them get through the mission. Not a good way to ensure longevity."

"What did you think was your very worst mission?" Kristin asked him.

"The one to Merseburg on November 2, 1944. Heaviest flak I've seen over any target." He referred to his notes. "We got hit by fighters. Lost 41 bombers and shot down 208 fighters, according to the papers."

"How many fighters did you say you shot down?" I asked.

"The papers gave us credit for 208, but don't believe that. If we hit one, three or four fellas would say they hit it. The problem was, it was just a big furball up there. It was hard to say who actually got that plane, unless you were the only guy shooting when the plane blew up in front of you."

He read from his old log entries.

"Let's see, Mission 15, November 5, 1944—target Ludwigshaven. Roughest flak yet. We got more flak holes here than ever before. No. 3 engine badly hit, losing oil all the way home, gas leak somewhere, nearly out of gas upon arrival to base, unable to land because of terrible weather."

He looked up and said, "We had to land at an emergency divert base. We got back to our own base four hours later, but we'd already been listed as missing in action. We immediately went to check our belongings, and all but the tail gunner's gear was intact. The grave robbers hadn't gotten to most of us yet, but the tail gunner, Harvey, was missing seven pairs of boxer shorts. And those things were near and dear in the Army because you couldn't get any more. There just weren't any available. I remember writing back to my wife here in the States, 'Please buy me some boxer shorts.' She wrote back, 'What are those? We're rationed over here.'"

"So the first thing people do when they hear somebody's missing in action," I asked, "is go and steal their belongings?"

"That's right. So Harvey was missing seven pairs of shorts. He didn't say a word. We were all armed with Colt .45 automatics in shoulder holsters, and he still had his on. He didn't say a word, just turned around and walked out the door. Came back quite some time later and laid six pairs of shorts down on his bed and checked them. Yeah, they had his ID on them. So he packed them away. He said, 'I couldn't find the seventh pair.'

"Next day I ran into somebody from another flight crew, and he said, 'What the hell's the matter with that tail gunner of yours? That man's crazy. He came into our hut waving a loaded .45 and ordered us to lay our shorts down on the bunk where he could see them!' And that's how he got his underwear back.

"November 16, 1944. Flew to the Duren area. Our mission was to support ground troops who'd asked for air support. No fighters or fighter-bombers were available, so they sent the whole damn 8th Air Force's heavy bombers to clear out this one target. I'll just read this to you: No. 1 engine out at 12,000 feet in initial climb—" He looked up. "This is right after takeoff. So the mission didn't start well."

He continued to read. "Never even assembled because weather was so bad. Forced to land at RAF Carnaby in Northern England after mission."

He said, "We were trying to get back to our own base at Deopham Green, but the weather had the base totally socked in. We contacted the control tower and they said, 'Can't land here.' We'd already heard. Between 600 and 700 four-engine bombers were flying around up there, all in overlapping traffic patterns, trying to land. Engines out, wounded on board, flak damage, everybody screaming for priority. They said, 'Don't even try to let down, you can't see, stay up at 22-23,000 feet where you can still see a little bit.' It was twilight.

"The tower said, 'Orbit the base while we find a divert base for you.' We said, 'Better hurry up because we're flying on fumes up here. In a minute we're going to have to land whether you like it or not. Should we turn around, head to the Channel, and bail out?'

"They said, 'Hold it, we got a divert base for you.' They gave us the coordinates. The navigator said, 'It's damn near a hundred miles! Do we have enough gas?'

"The flight engineer and pilot and copilot got together and decided we didn't have a choice. So we headed in that direction. We started letting down, trying to find a hole in the clouds, but it was solid.

"Finally the navigator said, 'We should be over it if my dead reckoning is right. Let's let down and see.' Johnson said, 'We gotta let down either way, we're running out of fuel.'

"He called down to me, sitting in the nose bubble, 'Hey Tex, you can see out the front better than I can, so if you see something ahead call it out.' So I looked and looked, and I saw something whip by. *Fffft!* And then I saw another one. *Fffffft!* Then I realized they were *trees*. And they were higher than we were. Not especially tall trees, just little ones. I screamed at Johnson, and he said, 'I got it. I got it. Can you find the runway?'

"I stared hard through the fog. A faint red glow appeared, and suddenly the fog thinned just enough to give me some visibility, and I said, 'Got the runway!'

"Johnson said, 'I see it.' Carnaby was a British emergency landing base equipped with FIDO, which stands for 'Fog, Intensive Dispersal Of.' It was a system of gas pipes running along either side of the runway. They lit the gas to burn off the fog. And that was what created the slight clearing that allowed us to see.

"The first time the pilot lined up to land I had to scream, 'Pull up! Pull up!' Because we were headed across the runway instead of down it. He pulled up, but didn't dare go too high off the ground because we'd be right back in the soup. He said, 'OK I've got the heading now,' and he turned around and took us down the runway.

"I looked out ahead and saw a British Lancaster bomber sitting in our path. It had crashed on landing in the middle of the runway about one third of the way down, right at our preferred touchdown point. It was burning and RAF personnel were down there shooting red flares and waving us off. They shouted at us over the radio to go away, and finally we just pulled the plug on it.

"We went around and he called them back and said, 'I'm coming down. I've got to land. I'm out of fuel.' They responded, 'You can't land *blah blah blah*.'

"Johnson told us, 'Stand by, we're going in. I don't even have enough fuel to get us to altitude so we can bail out. Tex, you stay down at the nose and call it out.'

"Everybody except the ball turret gunner stayed in position. We got down to it, and those trees started whipping by me on either side. From where I was sitting, it looked like we would barrel right into this Lancaster. All of a sudden Johnson pushed over and touched down just before we got there, bounced up over the Lancaster, and touched down on the other side. The Brits back there were just going nuts.

"As we rolled, Johnson shouted that he didn't have any brakes. The hydraulics were damaged. A barbed wire fence at the other end of the runway came up awfully fast. We went through it into a sugar beet field. As usual in England it was raining so the field was wet and muddy. The plane slid out into the field, dug into the mud, tipped over onto its nose, and broke the nose bubble out. Remember, I was sitting right there in the nose as all this happened. Then the plane flopped back down.

"To this day they claim I swung out of the nose and stood there in front of the plane shaking my fist up at the pilot, shouting 'You dumb SOB, when are you going to learn how to land this airplane?'

"We saw a house a little to the left of us. A group of people stood on the porch, watching us. As soon as I stood up and turned around and held my fist up like that, they all disappeared into the house. The Brits from the airfield came and picked us up, pulled the airplane back onto the runway, and towed us to a parking spot. They told us, 'Come on back with us and we'll put you up for the night.'

"We signed in to their barracks. Their chow wasn't the best I've ever had, so we asked if there was a town nearby. 'Yeah, there's a little town, Carnaby.' We asked if we could go take a look and they said sure.

"The only clothes we had with us was our flight gear. We walked up to the front gate and told the guard what we wanted, and he said, 'There'll be a bus along here in a minute. Just get on and tell the driver you want to get off at the nearest pub.' So we got on one of those double-decker buses. Lo and behold, there's ten of us, none older than twenty-six, and that bus was jam-packed with young ladies."

He responded to Kristin and Gisela's loud laughter with a wide grin.

"The ladies stared at us sitting there in our flight gear. One was bold enough to ask what we were doing there, and we told her we wanted to go to a pub. She said they were going into town to a dance right across the street from a pub, so they'd tell us when to get off the bus. She asked, 'Are you Canadian?' No. 'Australian?' No. 'Well what the hell are you?'

"I just unzipped the jacket and pulled it down, and there's that 8th Air Force patch. From that point on we got the red carpet.

"We went to the pub and then at only 8:30 at night, we heard, 'Time, time, if you please gentleman, time.' We'd had just enough beer to get going, and we certainly weren't ready to go back to that base out there. So somebody said, 'Didn't that gal tell us they were going to a dance across the street? Let's go over and see what's going on.'

"We walked over, and we hadn't really grasped the fact that the only males in this village were young kids and old men. Everybody else was off to war. We went in there and saw these girls dancing with one another! And that was just unacceptable.

"But," he said with a noble air, "I was married . . ."

Gisela and Kristin burst into laughter. "Yeah, right! Give me a break."

"What was her name again?" Kristin asked.

"Totally platonic, right?" Gisela needled him.

"It was a platonic friendship," he said, waving them off. "We had on our fleece-lined flight boots, and three pairs of socks, and heated boots inside. We couldn't dance that way so we took them off. The heated boots had wires running through the bottom of them, and we couldn't dance on those, so we got down to one pair of socks and danced the night away until 10 o'clock, and they started playing 'America'! You know, 'My country 'tis of thee!'

"So I told her, 'Come on, let's dance.' She said, 'No, no, this is the last dance.' I asked her, 'Why are they playing 'America?' She said, 'That's not 'America.' That's 'God Save the King'!

"So I put my boots back on and the ten of us started converging again. Barbera, this sweet young thing I'd been dancing with, looked soulfully into my eyes and said, 'I say, are you fixed up for the night?'

"Kind of caught me off guard. She must have seen the look on my face and said, 'No, no. My mother—' she turned and pointed toward an old lady across the room. 'We know what the living conditions are like out at that base, and my mother told me to ask two of you to come stay with us for the night.'

"So I turned around to the radio operator, 'cause he was twenty-six so he must know all about this sort of thing, and asked him if he'd like to go with me. He said, 'No, I'm going with that one over there.'

"I went to their house in the nearby village of Bridlington, and the little old lady fixed up a delicious meal for us. We just ate and ate and ate. This girl's sister was eight months, three weeks, and five days pregnant, at *least*. Her husband was in the RAF and had been shot down a few weeks earlier, and she'd just gotten word that he was in a German prison camp. The next morning the old lady made a nice breakfast. Then I met up with my crew and we found transportation home.

"Back at Deopham Green, we reported in, and the debriefing officer demanded, 'You mean you stayed with these people and ate with them instead of staying on the RAF base?' And we were all guilty.

"He said, 'All of you, this is an order. Next time you get a pass, you come to me, because you're going back up there, and you're going to take some stuff that I have for you to take. And that is an order. I'll put it in writing if I have to.'

"The next time we got a 72-hour pass, we dutifully reported in to him. He wrote out something and said, 'You go down to the mess hall and pick up this stuff from the mess sergeant.' Then he pulled out page after page of ration stamps. 'Take these, go to the PX, and get all the cigarettes you can buy.' And that's what we took with us when we went back up there. I looked around the town and found her in the shoe store she'd mentioned she worked for.

"I went back to her house with her that night. I had two fresh oranges from the base; they'd just gotten a shipment in. I gave her mom a bunch of ration stamps; I don't remember how many, but she was well overpaid. I also gave the old lady a bunch of cigarettes, and she took one and walked outside and came back in a little bit later and said, 'That was the best smoke I've had since 1939.'

"Her sister came walking by, her big old belly sticking out, still hadn't had the baby. So I gave her one of the oranges. She didn't say much, just said 'Thank you' and walked out. Later she came back in the room rubbing her belly and said, 'The baby and I thank you.' It turned out that was the first fresh orange she'd had since 1939."

He looked through his logs some more.

"Christmas Eve, 1944. The Battle of the Bulge had started on December 7. Bad weather had grounded all flights since December 11. Christmas Eve was the first day the weather broke, and by then the ground forces were in deep yogurt out there, so orders came out: 'If it's got wings, fly it. Just *go*.'

"We had two extra squadrons with us that had been forced to land at our base due to the bad weather, so we put up six squadrons that day. I flew with a new crew. My regular crew was one of fifty wounded planes on the way back; a fighter hit them. My radio operator was hit. And I saw an old friend of mine blow up from a direct flak hit."

He read from his logs. "Chin turret out, ball turret out, interphone out. Bomb bay had to be cranked open, engineer and radio operator passed out in the bomb bay from trying to crank the doors open. Copilot rescued them. Pilot passed out once. We finally salvoed the bombs over a small village near the target area."

He looked up. "It was just a tiny little village, but these buildings were a legal target because they were right next to a railroad track. I saw five or six houses on one side of the railroad track and lined up on those suckers and triggered the bombs. We were carrying 500-pound incendiary bombs. I saw at least two houses catch fire. My tail gunner was back there shouting, 'Burn you bastards, burn! Merry Christmas! Burn, you sons of bitches!' He said every house on that side of the street caught fire.

"We landed out of gas. A plane carrying my best friend, one of the group of four toggleers I told you about, came in on final approach, almost out of gas, and another plane came in from the side and tucked in front of him. The pilot saw it and pulled up, stalled out, and ran out of gas. All four engines just quit. The plane came down and hit on the nose and tumbled down the runway. Six of them were killed, and my best friend was sitting up there in the nose. They said they couldn't find enough of him to put in a mess kit.

"I flew my first mission on September 19, 1944, and exactly five months later, February 19, 1945, I flew my last mission." He closed the folder.

"Tell him about flying in the plane last year," Kristin said.

"We went over to England for a veterans reunion," he said. "Went to Norwich and Deopham Green, then crossed the channel to Cherbourg, got on the bus to go to Paris. Between Cherbourg and Paris, there's a little town called

Honeville. One man on the bus had been shot down in September of 1943 right over Honeville. The airplane blew up in front of him, and when he came to he was floating through the clouds so he pulled the ripcord. He no idea how high he was. He landed in a field right outside of town and a five-year-old girl was the first one to find him.

"Word got out in Honeville that this man was on this bus. And the town wanted to have a celebration and wanted him to be there. Would we mind stopping by there?

"We drove down a tiny cattle trail that passed for a road, entered the town, and saw people on foot, in cars, on bicycles, in World War II jeeps, armored personnel carriers, tanks out in a field, all that equipment was in better shape than when we left it there.

"That five-year-old girl was now a woman in her fifties. The pilot was the guest of honor. We went to a ceremony and saw a B-17 fly over. Then they held a banquet for us. I saw three men in flight suits, and I said to Kristin, 'Get that table over there with those people.'

"I had guessed correctly that they were the crew of that B-17. They couldn't speak English and my French was less than nothing, but we managed to communicate, and I finally figured out this one guy was flight engineer on a B-17 called the Pink Lady. I told them I'd been in the war, and one of them asked, 'Did you fly missions? How many?' I couldn't figure out how to say thirty-three, so I wrote it down. He saw that, turned to the others, and they started talking rapidly in French.

"We talked some more, and when we got ready to leave, a lady named Micheline came over to me and said, 'The four of you, when you see me leave, just follow me out. We can only handle four of you.' She took us over to a young Frenchman waiting by a car and told us, 'Go with him, we will take you to your destination. Don't worry, we've cleared it with your tour director, we will get you to Paris.'

"We climbed in the car, and I think that may have been the most exciting part, riding with a wild-eyed Frenchman down those little country roads. He took us to a little air-field out in the middle of nowhere. And there's the Pink Lady sitting right there. There's the flight crew. They ask if we'd like to fly to Paris with them!

"I took a deep breath and went up to the pilot. I asked him, 'How many flight hours have you got? Not necessarily on a B-17, but total?' He screwed up his face and thought for a while and said, '18,000.'

"I grinned and said, 'Sure, I'll fly anywhere with you.' He said, 'But my copilot is a rookie. He's only got 15,000.'

"We learned the Pink Lady was originally with the 447th Bomb Group and had flown six combat missions before the war ended and then was given to the government of France. This group had restored the plane to flyable condition, and they'd been flying it all over Europe to air shows. It's one of the planes used in the making of the film *Memphis Belle*.

"They put us all back in the waist and had us sit there for takeoff. When we got airborne, the flight engineer asked me, 'Would you like to sit in your original position?' So I went on up there real quick and got up there in the bombardier's chair. Here comes my Aggie son; first thing he does is raise his head and hit the sheet of metal that used to hold the radio up above and cut his head. So in all the pictures we have of the trip he's got this big bandage on his head. But I think Kristin enjoyed the flight."

"Oh, yeah," Kristin said, beaming. "I got to climb all over, cockpit, nose, everywhere."

"We approached Orly Airport in Paris," Stan said, "and flew by the Eiffel Tower, listening to the conversation over the radio with the control tower. It was in French, but this is what they said: 'B-17G tail number so and so, at such and such position requesting permission to land.'

"And without missing a beat the controller said, 'Say again aircraft type?'

"They weren't used to seeing B-17s!"

After the interview, the four of us went outside to Stan's workshop, where he and Gisela had been working together on a project. She held up a B-17 fuselage, made of balsa wood, that had to be nearly three feet long. On a worktable the intricate beginnings of a B-17 wing, the bottom surface and the ribs, sat over a set of blueprints.

"We've been working on this for months," Stan said. "It's presenting some real challenges, for example how to successfully fabricate fiberglass engine cowls."

"We're going to put motors in this," Gisela said.

"That's right, we fly these things," Stan said.

"You actually fly beautiful models like this?" I asked. "Aren't you afraid you'll destroy it?"

He shrugged.

"He did crash a really nice one once," Gisela said. "I felt so bad; he'd just finished building it!"

"It got out of range of the remote control," he explained.

We chatted about their hobby for a while and then I took my leave.

Two people from totally opposite ends of a vicious war, now happy in each other's company and quietly spending their days building things together.

There's got to be a message in there somewhere.

Gisela Botzenmayer holds the fuselage of a model B-17 she is helping Stan Prather to build.

Gisela Botzenmayer and Stan Prather today.

David Perkins
Fort Worth

"**M**y family moved to Fort Worth from Arkansas in the summer of 1941," David Perkins told me. "My father, Oscie Perkins, had grown up in Springtown, about 25 miles northwest of Fort Worth. So he was kind of coming back home. And that's where we were living when the war started for the United States in December of 1941.

"I don't remember a whole lot of it because I was four years old when the war started. But I remember the two-tone shoes the men wore!" He chuckled.

It took me a moment, but I got it.

"I remember later in the war I used to save tinfoil off the back of chewing gum wrappers and ball it up to give to the war effort. We collected scrap metal and turned it in. Those were very patriotic things to do. Everybody had food stamps. I was really impressed that I had a book of food stamps myself, with my name on it."

"Oh, you had your own at that age?"

"Yes, even at that age. Everybody had one. A few years later, after the war was over, I traded my book of food stamps with a little kid down the street for a little sailboat

Young David Perkins goes shopping with his sisters, Mary (left) and
Virginia, on West Seventh Street in downtown Fort Worth in 1943.

that he had. My parents weren't too happy about that, so they nullified that transaction.

"There were stamps for shoes, sugar, meat. We had Meatless Tuesdays, but my mother, Helen, was a great cook and always came up with something good. I remember people coming to our back door during that time too. Old drifters and tramps with unkempt beards. They'd come up through the alleyway and they would knock on the back door and say they were hungry. I remember this happening many times. And my mom would fix them food. My mother was one of the most generous people I've ever met in my life."

How long has it been since people allowed the homeless to knock on their doors and ask for food? What would happen if one tried something like that today?

"After my brother Joe was killed, I remember there was a woman down the block from us on East Jefferson in Fort Worth, who said, 'I don't hate Hitler. I just hate his ways.' I was a little kid and I went around telling people that the lady down the street hated Hitler's waves. I didn't understand what it was all about.

"Downtown Fort Worth was very crowded back then. We'd go shopping and have lunch there in one of the department stores or a little restaurant. People would be waiting for tables, and they'd just hover over you as you were eating, because there weren't enough places. And something you don't see now, we'd share a table with people we didn't know. I remember we sat in a booth with a man who had palsy, and he just about scared me to death with his shaking. My mother told me later it was OK, he just had a medical problem."

"Did your mother work?"

"Yes, she worked nights at Firestone Tire and Rubber during my first year in grade school. She'd come home early in the morning, fix me breakfast, and see me off. I'd walk by myself to school. My mother would turn the shades down and go to bed."

"How many brothers and sisters did you have?"

"I was the youngest, then my brother Oscie Jr., my sisters Mary and Virginia, and Joe was the oldest."

"Is the house you used to live in still there?"

"Yes, it's 1005 East Jefferson. My wife and I went by there three or four years ago. A black woman was out in the front yard. The neighborhood used to be completely white and now it's completely black. I stopped and said hello and told her, 'You know, I used to live in that house when I was a little bitty boy.' She said firmly, 'Well it's my house now!' I guess she took it the wrong way.

"One thing happened in downtown Fort Worth that made a big mark on me, in one of the department stores downtown, Monnig's or Stripling's, I'm not sure. I remember seeing two water fountains. One of them said 'Whites only' and the other said 'Coloreds only.' I was only five years old. And I just thought that was so unfair. Black people appeared OK to me."

"Well, sometimes kids are smarter than adults," I said.

"Kids don't carry around the baggage that adults do. We have predetermined ideas about what people are like. I think several hundred years from now maybe we'll get away from prejudice. I wish it could happen in my lifetime, but it won't.

"I had a lot of heart-to-heart discussions with my big sister Mary, and sometimes we used to talk about what we would do if we were black and had a lot of money. We came to the conclusion that we would move out on a big ranch way out where nobody could bother us.

"I remember going to church and seeing patriotic plays put on by the church groups all the time. Young men were up on stage behind sandbags, portraying soldiers fighting the war. Lightbulbs hung over them, and to imitate bombs exploding they would turn the lights on and off.

"I listened to the radio a lot. I liked Hap Harrigan, a leather-jacketed guy with a white silk scarf who flew a P-40. Brought to you by Grape Nuts Flakes. I listened to Superman, Captain Midnight, Captain Marvel. I sent off for decoder rings and things like that.

"I had a cardboard cutout set of a military camp. It came in a cardboard sheet. You'd punch out the pieces and put Tab A into Hole B and so forth, and you'd build tanks, armored cars, things like that.

"For Christmas of '43 or '44, I was going to get a little red wagon. They were being made out of wood then instead of metal. My parents couldn't get it in time, so instead I got a letter from Santa Claus. I failed to recognize my mother's handwriting at the time. It said something like 'Dear David, I'm sorry I couldn't get your wagon to you in time, but I'll have it to you in the middle of January. My elves will bring it to you.' And I memorized that letter. My teacher had me stand up in front of the class and recite that letter. I knew it by heart. It was a big thing to the other kids, too. Santa Claus wrote David a note! And sure enough in the middle of January, here comes a little red wagon.

"My mother and I would travel up to McGehee, a little town in Arkansas, to visit one of her sisters, my Aunt Bert, from time to time. Aunt Bert had a son in the service too. He flew PBYs in the Navy.

"Aunt Bert was kind of emotional. Once she came screaming through the house, 'Jimmy's dead, Jimmy's dead, Jimmy's dead!' Well, Jimmy was just fine. He made it home after the war.

"One time during one of those visits I was riding a bus with two cousins into McGehee. They lived outside of town, and McGehee was the big city to them. We passed by a place out in the middle of nowhere with a sign that said Japanese Internment. We could see the gates of a big camp.

"At the time I didn't give it much thought. See, I thought the drinking fountains in downtown Fort Worth were unfair, but we were at war with the Japs so I didn't give that any ethical thought at the time.

"Some time in the early '90s, my wife and I were up there driving around on a vacation, and we found a little obelisk there, a monument to the Japanese prisoners.

"While we stopped to look at it, a Japanese man about my age came up and told me he had lived in that camp! He had a tear in his eye. And I did too! Because I was out free, riding by the camp in a bus, and he was stuck in there behind the barbed wire fence. But he didn't harbor any anger over it, and I didn't harbor any guilt. It was just something that happened because of war.

"Joe was killed in February of '43. Before the war he'd been working for Kimbell Mills in Fort Worth. But as soon as he got old enough to enlist he did, in 1942. The only time he came back home was when he went AWOL from

Sheppard Air Force Base in Wichita Falls and hitchhiked down to see us in Fort Worth. He stood in the living room and taught me close order drill. My parents had given me a little soldier's uniform, and I wore mine and he wore his and he taught me how to march. I held a stick in place of a rifle.

"I remember very vividly when his plane, a B-17, went missing. We didn't have a telephone so we had to go across the street to the neighbors' house to use theirs, and the War Department let my parents know. His plane was missing for ten days, and finally they found it in the mountains of Washington. His crew had been in training, just about ready to go to over to England. All ten of them were killed.

"My mother just cried and cried. My father tried to comfort her. Everybody sat up in the living room, looking blank. I remember seeing a real awkward smile on Mary's face. I think we kids were a little embarrassed because we'd never seen our parents cry before. My father was very stoic. Life had kicked him around a little bit by then. In Arkansas he had owned a very large lumber mill that he'd inherited from his uncle. He'd been in World War I and then his uncle put him through bookkeeping school. When his uncle died he took over the Perkins Brothers Lumber Mill. It lasted until 1940 and then went broke, and that's why we moved to Fort Worth. My parents had always had a fair amount of money during the Depression, got a new car every year. Then when he went broke it kind of took the wind out of his sails. He never really recovered, never had a great amount of money after that.

"He would read me poetry. He was a real nice guy. But he didn't show a whole lot of feelings.

David Perkins' older brother Joe in 1942.

Walla Walla, Wash.
February 6, 1943

Dear Mother;

I'll take advantage of a quiet barracks to write just a little. There is hardly anyone here now. As it is Saturday night almost everyone has gone to town or to the show. I had seen the show and my blouse was in the cleaners so I stayed at home tonight. I guess that I should stay in every once in a while.

I am going to try to send $5 soon on the first. That should pay off the Red Cross. Then on April 1st I'll send the rest for the Training Command. I would send it next week, but I owe quite a bit around and about so can hardly afford to.

You know that I got quite a raise last month. My base pay jumped from

$78⁰⁰ per month to $96⁰⁰. That's not too bad. Totaled with my flying pay of $48⁰⁰ I make $144⁰⁰ per month. And that is clear. That's better than I was doing as a civilian. Of course it goes just as fast as if I was making $50⁰⁰. If I was married I would draw $37⁵⁰ more. Seems to me like that's a money-making proposition.

This is the worst camp that I have hit as far as privileges are concerned. We are treated like a bunch of prize rookies here. If we weren't Instructor Crews we would be treated much worse. The thing that gets me more than anything else is the furlough situation. We are allowed one 7 day furlough while here. On that furlough one can only travel 750 miles. Why that would only get me about as

far as Salt Lake City which wouldn't
do me any good at all. I may throw
discretion to the winds and go
home anyway. However I would
be a private soon after, but it
would be worth it. Yet again
I may go to Seattle and throw
the biggest bender that town
has ever seen. I don't know hardly
what to do.

I was plenty mad last week
two days before we left Sioux
City. We went down to Operations
to fly early one morning. When
we got there we were told our
mission was to fly to San
Antonio, Texas and back "non-stop".
Well we did. We flew to San Antonio
and back non-stop. We flew
right over Gainesville, Denton
Sherman, and then Dallas. I did

everything, but bail out there.
Off in the distance as we flew
over Dallas I could see a smudge
on the horizon that was Fort
Worth. Well it broke my heart, but
I'm coming home sometime.
The sun was sure warm on the
plane down around that part of
the country after leaving the
frigid North. Maybe I can make
that trip again. Next time I'll
bail out. We came back to
Sioux City the same day and
never stopped. It was nearly
4,000 miles worth of flight.
Well I had better close now
From your disgruntled son.
Love to all

Joe

Joe Perkins' last letter to his mother before dying in a plane crash.

302

David Perkins' parents, Oscie and Helen, circa 1921.

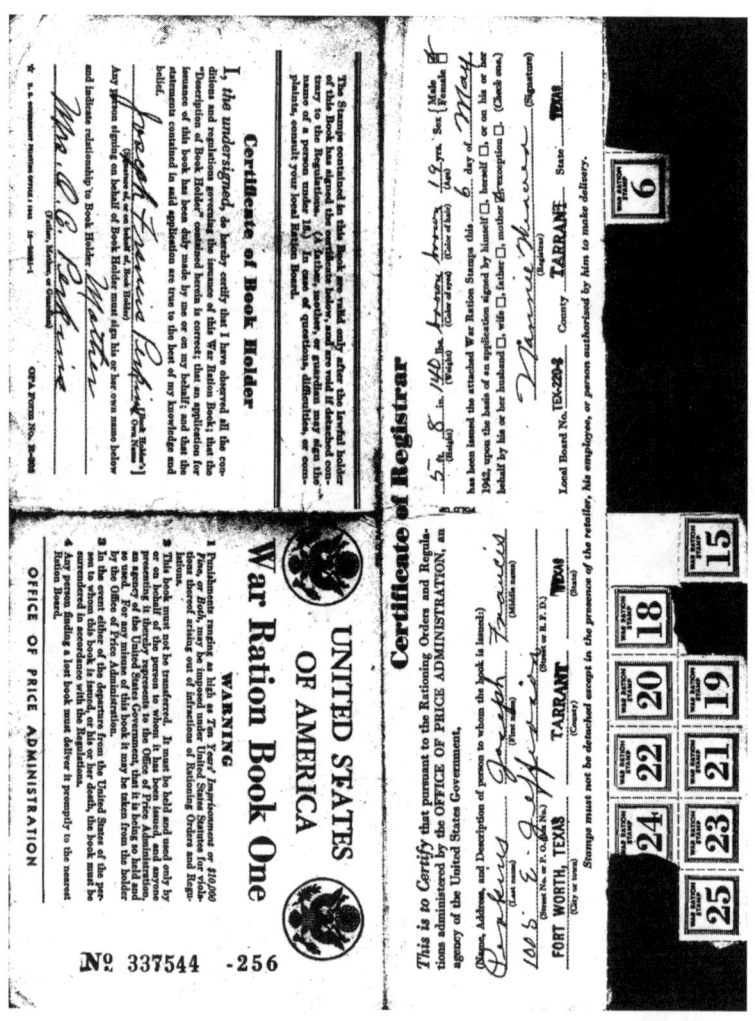

Book of ration stamps that belonged to David Perkins' brother Joe.

"Times after that I would catch my mother in the bedroom kneeling down and praying by the bed. She put a gold star in the window."

He stopped talking for a moment. I waited.

"Talking about Joe," he said, "there are still times when I stop and think, 'What would my life be like if I still had this other big brother? Would he have been a senator from the state of Texas? Would my life have been enhanced? Or would he have been an alcoholic and I would have had to take care of him? To this day I still ask what would have happened if Joe had come back. Would my life be better, worse, or the same?"

"Were you ever personally frightened because of the war?" I asked. "The thought that maybe the Germans or Japanese would come?"

"I never felt fear during World War II," he said firmly. "I felt very secure as a kid. Our parents, for all their faults, must have been doing something right.

"It was different during the Cold War; I'd see an airplane and wonder, did the Russians get a bomber through? But I never felt fear during World War II. It never occurred to me that we could lose, and I think the adults felt the same way. That may be why we won. Americans don't have a concept of losing a war and losing our way of life. Even when we lost the Vietnam War, that wasn't on our home ground. We were still free. I don't think we can ever be beaten at home.

"We used to go out to Springtown a lot and spend time out there. I had a cousin who lived there, Wayne Smith, who was taken prisoner of war by the Germans in Italy in 1943. He was a medic. His unit was pulling back during a German counterattack, a kid got wounded, and Wayne went back to get him. And Wayne got wounded too, and the Germans captured both of them. Wayne nursed the other guy back to health. Without him, the kid would have died. My aunt, Lela Smith, had another son in the war too, so she had two silver stars in her window.

David Perkins' cousin Wayne in 1940.

"Aunt Lela would make knitted gloves and things to put in a Red Cross package to send to Wayne. I wrote letters to him, and he got them and wrote letters back to me.

"Springtown back then, we're talking three blocks. It had a post office and an icehouse right down the street from my aunt's house, with a one-lung compressor that made the ice. That thing used to scare me all night long going *flump, flump, flump.* They had a movie theater there too, so we'd go down and see Roy Rogers, Johnny Mac Brown, Gene Autry.

"It was a great little place to visit. It was not integrated at all, though. There were no black people, none whatsoever. You know, I never got to go to school with black kids, and I always felt like I was kind of cheated. I never got to know any black people very well personally until I went into the Marine Corps in the 1950s.

"My Uncle Joe Smith, Lela's husband, passed away about a month before my brother died. My parents wouldn't let me go to either funeral. I stayed with the people across the street while my brother's was going on. But I was very much aware that he was gone, he wasn't coming back. I understood the concept of death. I knew that we were fighting the Germans and the Japanese, and I knew men were dying."

"My cousin Wayne never got a parade when he came home after the war. I'll never forget his homecoming. It was a very hot day in the middle of summer. I was staying with my aunt in Springtown when Wayne returned. She had a car up on blocks in a dusty garage behind the hen house where I used to get warm eggs in the morning. The wheels had been taken off, and Aunt Lela had somebody come by and put them back on. Aunt Lela couldn't drive as well as my mother, and my mother was an awful driver. But she drove that car down to meet Wayne, and we waited in the grueling heat as he came in on a Trailways bus.

Front and back of a postcard sent to David Perkins by his cousin Wayne Smith from a prisoner of war camp in Germany.

"Springtown didn't have a bus station. In fact back then none of its roads were paved except for the Jacksboro Highway, which ran through it. The bus just pulled over by the side of the road and then Wayne got off, wearing his uniform.

"Aunt Lela went over, crying, and welcomed him. No fanfare.

"Wayne already knew before he arrived that his father had died while Wayne was a prisoner of war. The three of us walked across the highway to the Springtown cemetery to visit his father's grave. Wayne carried me piggyback because there were stickers and it was kind of sandy. He stood over his father's grave, holding me on his back, and cried.

"That was his parade, me and his mom."

"To me, he was a hero."

David Perkins and his cousin Wayne Smith at a family reunion in 1992.

Index